THE WAVE 4 WAY

TO BUILDING

YOUR

DOWNLINE

Books by Richard Poe:

Wave 3
The Wave 3 Way
The Einstein Factor
Black Spark, White Fire
Wave 4

For more information about Richard Poe
and the *Wave* books, see these Web sites:

www.richardpoe.com
www.buywave4.com

Richard Poe

The
WAVE 4
WAY

to Building
Your Downline

PRIMA SOHO
An Imprint of Prima Publishing
3000 Lava Ridge Court • Roseville, California 95661
(800) 632-8676 • www.primalifestyles.com

Library of Congress Cataloging-in-Publication Data
Poe, Richard
        The wave 4 way to building your downline / Richard Poe.
        p.   cm.
        ISBN 0-7615-2213-1
        1. Leadership. 2. Selling. 3. Marketing. I. Title: wave four way to building your downline. II. Title.
HD57.7.P64 2000
658.4'092—dc21   00-062333

00 01 02 03 HH 10 9 8 7 6 5 4 3 2 1
Printed in the United States of America

How to Order
Single copies may be ordered from Prima Publishing, 3000 Lava Ridge Court, Roseville, CA 95661; telephone (800) 632-8676 ext. 4444. Quantity discounts are also available. On your letterhead, include information concerning the intended use of the books and the number of books you wish to purchase.

Visit us online at www.primalifestyles.com

To my wife, Marie

CONTENTS

FOREWORD

Richard Poe is the most captivating and widely published writer in the history of the network marketing industry. The body of material and the breadth and depth of industry coverage he has produced over the last decade has been spectacular!

In 1990, when I launched my research on the network marketing industry at the University of Illinois at Chicago, I conducted the classic academic "literature search" of the business press. There was virtually no descriptive or analytical information about network marketing and very limited coverage of direct selling in the business periodical literature or marketing textbooks.

Industry information that was available was largely commercial advertising and focused on distributor recruiting, company products, trade press coverage of industry personalities, and motivational, usually unsubstantiated, "rags to riches" personal testimonials.

Enter Richard Poe's classic article, "Network Marketing: The Most Powerful Way to Reach Consumers in the '90s," published in *Success* magazine, May 1990, which opened the publishing floodgates for network marketing. John Milton Fogg has reported that article to be "the single most copied and widely distributed essay in the history of magazine publishing."

Then in the early '90s, Richard Poe published *Wave 3* and *The Wave 3 Way*, presenting an overview of the industry's history and current infrastructure. In 1999, *Wave 4:*

Network Marketing in the 21st Century was published, which updated the *Wave* series and reviewed how network marketing can be interconnected with the age of the Internet.

Initiating the year 2000, Richard Poe has written another industry milestone, *The Wave 4 Way to Building Your Downline*. *The Wave 4 Way* focuses on the leadership skills required to build a successful downline distributor organization in the twenty-first century.

In *The Wave 4 Way*, Poe has adapted self-improvement and leadership concepts from a variety of references including Napoleon Bonaparte, Stephen Covey, Abraham Lincoln, the McDonald's Corporation, and H. Ross Perot, and has applied them to *network marketing business building*.

Richard Poe does a stellar job in focusing these concepts on case studies of real network marketing distributor leaders. The leaders featured are high-income producers with massive downline organizations that have a history of productive performance. They epitomize the leadership styles and skills that *The Wave 4 Way* recommends. Poe highlights paint-by-the-number strategies and tactics that network marketing practitioners can apply in their day-to-day businesses.

As a professor of marketing, I conclude in my professorial role: *The Wave 4 Way* is *required reading* for your network marketing education. It is fact-filled, informative, and very entertaining. Enjoy *The Wave 4 Way*.

—*Charles W. King*
professor of marketing,
University of Illinois at Chicago,
coauthor of *The New Professionals: The Rise of
Network Marketing As the Next Major Profession*

ACKNOWLEDGMENTS

Limited space allows me to thank only a small portion of the many people who have helped make the *Wave* books a success. I extend my deepest appreciation to all, both named and unnamed.

First and foremost, I thank my wife, Marie. Thanks also to Duncan Maxwell Anderson, Scott DeGarmo, John Milton Fogg, Ben Dominitz, Susan Silva, Charles W. King, Colby Olds, Jennifer Basye Sander, Leonard Clements, Rod Cook, Ridgely Goldsborough, Lloyd Jassin, and all the rest. Grateful acknowledgment is made to *House of Business* magazine, which published earlier versions of much of the material in chapter 15.

INTRODUCTION

Money is one of the greatest instruments of freedom ever invented by man," wrote economist Friedrich von Hayek in his 1944 masterpiece, *The Road to Serfdom*. The great thing about money, said von Hayek, is that you can spend it as you wish. It might even be argued that the ability to earn and spend money freely is the single quality that most clearly distinguishes a free man from a slave.

A slave has everything he needs to live: a roof over his head; clothes on his back; food to eat; medical care when he is sick. And, of course, he always has a job.

The one thing he lacks is choice. A slave does not have the option of saving up his money, so that he can one day tell his boss, "I quit." He cannot buy a different house if he tires of the first one. He cannot change doctors if the sawbones his master provides turn out to be incompetent. Whatever arrangements his master makes, the slave must accept.

Many people today have been deluded into thinking that they can rely on the government "safety net" to save them from poverty. But government handouts are not so different from slavery. Food stamps will only buy food. Housing credits will only buy housing. Medicaid will only pay for medical care. Like the slave owner, the dispenser of government relief reserves for himself the right to determine how your resources are spent.

As more and more jobs vanish through downsizing and technological change, people in the twenty-first century are faced with a hard choice. We can beg the government for relief—in effect, selling ourselves into slavery—or we can go out and earn our freedom the hard way, through entrepreneurship. This book was written for those men and women who choose the path of liberty.

We rightly honor men like George Washington who led their people to freedom through force of arms. But there is another kind of leader whose contribution to liberty is no less vital. He is the business leader, the entrepreneur.

The Wave 4 Way to Building Your Downline is a handbook for that special breed of freedom fighter—the network marketer—whose battleground is the decentralized, wired economy of the twenty-first century. Drawing from the wisdom of Xenophon, Napoleon, Sun Tzu, and other historic leaders, it instructs the ambitious networker in the timeless art of enlisting others to help you achieve your goals.

Here you will find practical instruction in how to inspire, teach, admonish, and persuade. Here are techniques for sharing your vision; for thinking positive; for building a team; and for delegating responsibility and raising up other leaders to help you.

The principles in this book can be applied to many fields. But there are few endeavors where they are likely to reap more tangible benefit than in building and sustaining a multilevel sales organization. Network marketing offers one of the most efficient and economical ways of attaining business ownership, residual income, and financial independence in the twenty-first century. I offer this book to those of you with the boldness to embrace the future. May it smooth your path and inspire you in difficult times.

—*Richard Poe*

The Path
of Leadership

CHAPTER 1

The Magic Moment

A sigh of relief escaped Steve Petroff's chest. Every part of his body seemed to relax, as if from a deep-muscle massage. "It's over," Steve told himself. "My struggle is finally over."

It seemed hard to believe, but the proof lay right there in front of him. Going over his account books that afternoon, Steve had calculated that his business now generated $1,000 per week in commissions. On the surface, it didn't seem like much. But it meant that Steve could quit his job and devote himself full time to building his business. "I realized that if I could make $1,000 a week, I could make $2,000 a week," Steve recalls. And he was right.

Steve's business was no ordinary enterprise. He had built a network marketing organization. Sometimes called multi-level marketing or MLM, network marketing is a system that allows independent sales representatives to work from home, recruiting other sales representatives and drawing commissions from the sales of their recruits (and from the recruits of their recruits and so on).

The total number of people you recruit into your organization is called your "downline." Build a large enough downline, and you can theoretically collect commissions from hundreds or even thousands of salesmen, many levels deep. That means you are earning money not only from your own efforts, but from other people's efforts as well. By this means, it is theoretically possible to build up a regular, residual income stream far greater than anything you could ever hope to earn through your personal sales efforts.

The MLM company that Steve had joined sold legal service coverage to individual and corporate clients. It was a great product that practically sold itself. But there are limits to the number of policies a single salesman can sell. His earning potential is determined by the number of calls he can personally make each day.

What got Steve excited about his $1,000 a week was the fact that only a small portion of it came from his personal sales. Most came from other people's work. Steve's multilevel business had the potential now to keep generating income for him, even when he personally did not

> **B**uild a large enough downline, and you can theoretically collect commissions from hundreds or even thousands of salesmen, many levels deep.

choose to make sales calls. He could take a day off, or even a week or a month, and his commissions would keep rolling in. His business might even grow larger while he was on vacation, because other people would keep working, in his absence, to win new customers and recruit new sales reps.

This already seemed to be happening in Steve's downline. Many of his recruits had begun exercising initiative in recent weeks. No longer content to wait for Steve's instructions, they were going out and building the network themselves. They held opportunity meetings in their local communities, recruiting and training new prospects. Steve's network had hosted nineteen such meetings across Indiana, just in the last week. Steve would have felt obliged to speak at each and every one of those nineteen meetings in the past. But this time around, he found it necessary to attend only one of them. Like a mother bird who sees her chicks take wing for the first time, Steve realized that his downline was finally starting to build the business on its own.

It was a magic moment for Steve Petroff—the moment when his MLM business began running on autopilot. From then on, his income began growing by leaps and bounds. New business no longer had to pass through the single, narrow bottleneck of Steve Petroff. It was being generated by many different people at once.

Only six months later, Steve found that his weekly income had doubled to $2,000. He was drawing over $100,000 in annual commissions by the end of the first year, and $230,000 by the end of the second. During six and a half years with Pre-Paid Legal Services, he and his wife, Nancy, earned more than $2.1 million. It had been a long, hard road for the Petroffs. Month after month, they had relied on little more than their faith in network marketing. But once they reached that Magic Moment, their faith was rewarded beyond all expectation.

Priming the Pump

Sales motivator Zig Ziglar likens the struggle for success to working an old-fashioned hand pump. Nowadays, if you want water, you just turn a faucet. But in the old days it took more effort.

First, you had to prime the pump. That meant pouring a little water into the top, to get the flow started. "Before you can get anything out, you must put something in," Ziglar explains in his book *See You at the Top*.

Next, you had to invest physical effort, pumping hard, for several minutes, as you drew the water up from deep underground. During that time, no water came from the spout. It was all work, with no reward.

Eventually, however, the water would reach the top. Everything changed at that point. Instead of all work and no reward, you got massive results with little effort. The slightest pressure on the handle would send water gushing from the spout. Slow, easy strokes were all you needed now, to keep the water flowing.

Building a business is like that. The start-up phase requires massive effort, with little payoff. But once your business turns profitable, the cash tends to keep flowing, even when you reduce the intensity of your work.

That's because of the power of leverage. Crudely defined, leverage means getting other people to do your work for you. In a conventional business, employees and managers carry the workload. In a multilevel marketing company, the work is done by a network of independent sales representatives. The more recruits you add to your downline, the less work you have to do personally.

Conventional businesses offer a rich source of leverage. But network marketing offers more. That's because, in an MLM organization, you gain access to the power of geometric growth.

According to mathematicians, a quantity grows geometrically when you multiply it over and over again by some other number. If, for instance, you took a penny, and doubled it every day (multiplied it by two), that penny would have multiplied to over $21 million by the end of the first month (assuming that the doubling began on day one).

> Once your business turns profitable, the cash tends to keep flowing, even when you reduce the intensity of your work.

Network marketing organizations benefit from the same phenomenon. Let's say you recruit five people in your first month. Now suppose that each of your five recruits goes on to recruit five more in the second month. Theoretically, if the process continued, month after month, with perfect precision—each recruit bringing in exactly five more people—you would have 19,530 sales reps (or "distributors") in your downline, after six months. That's a lot of leverage!

Of course, things do not always work so perfectly in the real world. Most of your recruits will drop out after a short time. Others will stay in the business but will fail to win any recruits of their own. In a real-life MLM organization, you'll need to do a lot of pumping before the water finally starts to flow.

But eventually, it will come. You just have to keep pumping. You will wake up one morning to find that your Magic Moment has arrived. Your downline will grow of its own accord. Your commissions will swell with each passing month. The power of leverage will be at your disposal. This book was written to show you how to get there.

CHAPTER 3

It's Not for Everyone

There are three types of people in a network marketing organization: leaders, distributors, and dropouts. The dropouts are the most numerous. They are the ones who will join your organization, then quit before accomplishing anything.

Distributors will stay in the organization, at least for a while. But they will contribute at a lower level. They may buy the product for their own personal consumption, staying in the organization simply to qualify for a wholesale discount. Or they may sell just enough product at retail to pay themselves back for their own purchases, thus breaking even.

A few may even take a stab at building the business. They will prospect for recruits and maybe sign a few people up. But most will not have the drive or persistence to keep going. Long before the water starts pouring from the spout, they will stop pumping. For them, the Magic Moment remains an unattainable dream.

The third and smallest category of network marketers are the leaders. These are the people who actually commit to building the business. They put in long hours prospecting for new recruits, then teaching those recruits to prospect. They keep working and never give up. Eventually, their downlines grow to the point where they begin generating substantial monthly income.

Only a few will become leaders in a network marketing organization. Most will be dropouts or ordinary distributors. In this respect, MLM is no different from any other business or endeavor.

More than a hundred years ago, an Italian economist named Vilfredo Pareto found that, in any given enterprise, about 20 percent of the people will gain 80 percent of the benefits of that enterprise.

A Marxist would say that the 20 percent are bourgeois oppressors who exploit the other 80 percent. But Pareto believed just the opposite. He believed that the 20 percent constituted an elite. Because they worked harder, dreamed bigger, and contributed more to the enterprise, they naturally gained more from it than the 80 percent who were less motivated and less productive.

> They call it the 80/20 Rule. Any experienced networker will tell you that 80 percent of the work is done by 20 percent of the people.

Few network marketers have ever heard of Vilfredo Pareto. But most are familiar with Pareto's Law, under a different name. They call it the 80/20 Rule. Any experienced networker will tell you that 80 percent of the work is done by 20 percent of the people.

Those 20 percent are the leaders. They are highly motivated, super-productive, and tirelessly persistent. They are an elite. It is the leaders who drive the business and set the pace. It is they who cause an MLM organization to grow.

If you wish to experience a Magic Moment in your own life, to achieve a continuous, self-renewing income stream, then you must steel yourself for a great struggle. Only by working harder than the rest can you earn your place among the 20 percent. Only by offering yourself as an example and a guide to others, can you walk the path of a leader.

CHAPTER 4

Leaders Are Made, Not Born

Leadership has an extraordinary power," says William A. Cohen, in *The Art of the Leader*. "It can make the difference between success and failure in anything you do. . . . Leadership has to do with getting things accomplished by acting through others. Regardless of your own abilities, there are many important goals that you cannot attain without the help of others."

One of those goals is building a network marketing downline. You will never succeed without help. And the only way to get other people's help is to provide compelling and powerful leadership.

"Easier said than done," some readers will grumble. For many of us, the word *leadership* conjures up unpleasant memories of high school, when other people, better endowed with looks, brains, or talent, always seemed to get the prize: the top girl or guy, the slot on the football team or cheerleading squad, the Ivy League scholarship. Those people were leaders. Not us.

We imagine that the potential for leadership lies in our genes. Some men are just born to be alpha males, we tell ourselves; some women to be alpha females. But centuries of experience have shown the fallacy of this belief.

"Just about anyone can become a competent leader," says Cohen. "The only thing you need to know is what to do and then to do it."

Cohen is a management professor at California State University at Los Angeles and a leading corporate consultant. But most of what he knows about leadership he learned in Vietnam, as an air commando, flying perilous night missions against enemy convoys. In later years, Cohen became a general in the Air Force Reserve.

Nowhere is leadership more critical than on the battlefield, where every decision means life or death. Military commanders cannot afford to put the wrong people in positions of responsibility. Stringent procedures and guidelines have been developed over the centuries to select and train the best leaders. Based upon this experience, military men such as William Cohen are unanimous in rejecting the myth of the "natural-born" leader. Cohen cites two great leaders, in this regard:

> The only way to get other people's help is to provide compelling and powerful leadership.

"I have read of men born peculiarly endowed by nature to be a general," remarked General William Tecumseh Sherman. "But I have never seen one."

President Dwight Eisenhower once told his son, "The one quality that can develop by studious reflection and practice is the leadership of men."

As on the battlefield, so in network marketing. The skills of leadership can be learned through "studious reflection and practice." Once mastered, they will empower you to achieve extraordinary things.

"The essence of leadership is very simple," Cohen explains. "It is to motivate people to perform to their maximum potential to achieve goals or objectives that you set."

CHAPTER 5

The
Wave 4 Way

Network marketing has gone through great changes in its fifty-five-year history. Readers familiar with my previous books know that I have divided MLM's evolution into four distinct phases, as follows:

Wave 1 (1945–1979)—The Underground Phase
Wave 2 (1980–1989)—The Proliferation Phase
Wave 3 (1990–1999)—The Mass Market Phase
Wave 4 (2000 and beyond)—The Universal Phase

Wave 1 was the industry's Wild West phase, when pyramid schemes thrived alongside legitimate companies, and government regulators made up the rules as they went along. Wave 2 began when PC technology made it possible to run a network marketing company from your desktop, and the number of MLM start-ups skyrocketed.

Then came Wave 3. New technology, such as fax-on-demand, satellite broadcasts, video prospecting, three-way phone calls, drop-shipping programs, and toll-free 800 numbers began to automate the business, making it easier for rank-and-file networkers to succeed. Wave 4 continued the automation process, and also introduced easier compensation plans, that made the business more accessible for ordinary networkers and part-timers. The advent of e-commerce and Web-based prospecting has opened the door for MLM's greatest expansion, into regions, markets, and industries where it had no previous foothold.

As network marketing merges with the Internet, corporate America has been forced to take notice. Many of the hottest new business strategies on the dot-com frontier borrow heavily from MLM.

For instance, affiliate or "viral marketing" programs—in which an e-commerce company, such as Amazon.com, encourages customers to become distributors of its product, via the Internet—draw directly on the MLM tradition. Many even offer true multilevel compensation plans, in which distributors recruit other distributors who recruit other distributors and draw commissions from the sales of several layers of recruits.

> Technology is a great tool, but it cannot eliminate the need to motivate, inspire, and guide your people to high achievement.

All of this has led to a kind of techno-giddiness among network marketers. Some have begun calling this affliction "Wave 4 fever." It means that everyone is searching for the next big innovation, the next Internet gimmick. More and more MLM companies seek to lure recruits with the promise of a fully automated business, conducted over the Internet, requiring no physical contact with customers and prospects.

But that is not the Wave 4 Way. Technology is a great tool, but it cannot eliminate the need to motivate, inspire, and guide your people to high achievement. The need for flesh-and-blood leadership is basic to human nature. Its methods have not changed fundamentally for thousands of years. In the age of the Internet, as people retreat more and more behind their computer screens, their need for leaders has grown stronger, not weaker.

In short, the Wave 4 Way is the way of leadership. It is a process by which you will push through the wall of Internet anonymity and reach the hearts and minds of your downline. Master it, and you will conquer the cyber-markets of tomorrow. Master it not, and the Internet may well conquer you.

PART

The Path of Leadership: Summary

THE MAGIC MOMENT

The Magic Moment occurs in every successful MLM downline. It is the moment when your downline becomes self-sufficient, because you have trained enough leaders to keep the business going without your constant, personal supervision.

PRIMING THE PUMP

Achieving the Magic Moment takes time and effort, much like using an old-fashioned hand pump to draw water from the ground. You have to do a lot of pumping before the water rises to the top and pours from the spout. Likewise, you have to work hard, for a long time, with little or no reward, before your Magic Moment comes.

THE 80/20 RULE

The 80/20 Rule—sometimes known as Pareto's Law—holds that 20 percent of the people in any enterprise will do 80 percent of the work. That same 20 percent will also receive 80 percent of the rewards. It is this 20-percent elite that constitutes the leadership of an MLM organization.

THE DEFINITION OF LEADERSHIP

"The essence of leadership," says management expert, career Air Force officer and Vietnam combat veteran William A. Cohen, "is to motivate people to perform to their maximum potential to achieve goals or objectives that you set." That is also the definition of success in MLM. To achieve a substantial residual income, you need to motivate other people to build your downline for you.

LEADERS ARE MADE, NOT BORN

"The one quality that can develop by studious reflection and practice is the leadership of men," said President Eisenhower, former Supreme Commander of Allied Forces in World War II. As on the battlefield, so in network marketing. The skills of leadership can be learned. You don't have to be born with them.

THE WAVE 4 WAY

In the Wave 4 era—the age of Web-based network marketing—more and more MLM companies seek to lure recruits with the promise of an automated cyber-business, requiring no face-to-face prospecting. But technology cannot eliminate the need to motivate, inspire and guide your people. In the depersonalized age of the Internet, the need for leaders has grown stronger, not weaker. The Wave 4 Way is the path of flesh-and-blood leadership.

PART TWO

THE WAVE 4 WAY

The Seven Traits
of an MLM Leader

CHAPTER 6

What Makes
a Leader?

Harland Sanders was a failure, by the world's standards. At age sixty-six, he was broke and out of work. It seemed a hard end to a hard life. Sanders had been fending for himself since age twelve. He had worked every kind of odd job and dabbled in many businesses. Only after suffering one failure after another, did Sanders finally succeed in eking out a meager living for himself and his family, running a gas station in the Kentucky mountains during the Great Depression.

Through hard work and persistence, Sanders managed to turn his cooking skills into a successful roadside restaurant whose fame soon spread around the state. But he'd hardly had time to get used to his new success when disaster struck. In the early '50s, a new superhighway diverted traffic away from his remote town. Sanders was ruined. At age sixty-six, when most men think of retiring, Sanders could look forward only to more hardship.

Sanders had a choice. He could have sunk into a quagmire of depression and self-pity. But instead, he rose to the challenge. He took on a role unlike anything that he had tried in his sixty-six years of life. Sanders became a leader.

Living on $105 a month in Social Security, he took to the road in an old, beat-up Cadillac. Sanders drove from one state to another, stopping at every restaurant he passed and offering to cook dinner for the owner. Once the restaurateur had tasted Sanders's special "Kentucky Fried Chicken," Sanders would make an offer. In exchange for the recipe, the restaurant owner would agree to pay the "Colonel" one nickel for every chicken he sold.

Barely ten years later, Sanders had built an empire of more than 600 franchises. His restaurant chain, Kentucky Fried Chicken, was bought out by PepsiCo in 1986 for $840 million. Sanders today is remembered as one of the great leaders of American business.

What is interesting about Sanders's story is how little inclination he showed, in his first sixty-six years of life, to become a national business leader. No doubt, the capacity for greatness was present in Sanders's character from an early age. But he lived most of his life without exploiting it. Only great desperation, brought on by the collapse of his business, motivated Sanders to take on the mantle of leadership.

> No matter how old you are or what you have accomplished in life so far, it is never too late to develop the capacity to lead.

Most of us are not so different from Sanders. The vast majority of us have done little, in our lives, to mark us as leadership material. Yet we have the capacity within us. All we need is a sufficiently compelling reason to switch into high gear.

For more and more people today, that stimulus is coming in the form of economic hardship. Corporations are downsizing. Taxes are rising. Competition is intensifying. Technology is accelerating. Business ownership and financial independence are no longer just attractive luxuries. They have become necessities in the twenty-first century. Only by building a residual income can we assure a stable life for ourselves and our families in the turbulent years to come.

In order to accomplish that, we must become leaders. We must cultivate the skill of motivating others to help us achieve our goals. Colonel Sanders didn't master these skills until he was sixty-six years old. No matter how old you are or what you have accomplished in life so far, it is never too late to develop the capacity to lead.

The first step is to work on yourself. To a much greater extent than we realize, the attitudes, habits, and emotional reflexes that make up our personalities come from outside us. They are impressed upon us early in life by parents, siblings, schoolmates, and teachers. Just as we learned one way of dealing with the world, we can learn another. If you do not yet have the character of a leader, you can still acquire it.

A leader is distinguished by certain unmistakable personality traits. All can be developed through "studious reflection and practice," as Eisenhower put it. The trick lies in knowing what those traits are. The following pages will teach you. Master the seven essential traits of an MLM leader and make them part of your soul. Before you know it, the habit of leading others will be as instinctive to you as eating and breathing.

CHAPTER 7

Trait Number 1— Drive

Today, Steve Petroff is cofounder and vice president of his own network marketing firm, Liberty Legal. But just a few years ago, he was on the brink of spiritual and financial ruin. His twelve-year-old cabinet business had gone under. At age forty-seven, Steve was faced with the prospect of starting life over from scratch. The problem was, he didn't know if he was up to the challenge.

"I pictured myself working at Walmart or McDonald's to support my retirement," Steve recalls. He sank into a deep depression. He puttered around the house for six months, fixing anything he could find that was broken. "By the time I was done, everything worked perfectly in our house," he says.

Everything, that is, except the household budget. Steve's wife, Nancy, worked as a bookkeeper. But, with two of their five children still in college, Nancy's $30,000 salary was not enough. The only relief came when a hailstorm destroyed two cars in their driveway. The insurance money arrived just in time to pay some critical bills. "We couldn't have survived without that," says Steve.

A WAKE-UP CALL

So deeply had he withdrawn from the world, Steve had lost sight of how his behavior affected others. One day he was forced to confront the problem, however. He and Nancy were sitting in the living room. Watching him from the couch, Nancy said, "Steve, you're starting to scare me."

No other words were necessary. Steve knew exactly what she meant. For six months, Nancy had watched him nurse his wounds. Now she was no longer sure that he was going to recover. "The last thing I ever wanted to do was scare her," Steve recalls. "It made me pop out of my coma."

Swallowing his pride, Steve went to see a longtime rival of his, the owner of a cabinet company with whom Steve had competed for twelve years. The man hired him as a salesman. It was quite a step down from owning his own company, but Steve was determined to do whatever it took to get back on his feet.

THE HUNGER

Like Colonel Sanders when his restaurant closed, Steve was driven by desperation. His intense need to recover his dignity and independence filled him with a mighty resolve to succeed.

Veteran network marketers have learned that a hungry recruit is the best recruit. Often, networkers deliberately seek out people who have suffered financial reverses and are struggling to regain control of their lives. Such people are powerfully motivated. Deep in their hearts, they have something to prove. They will not stop pushing until they have made their point.

I call this quality "drive." It is drive that gives MLM leaders their seemingly superhuman ability to overcome obstacles, slough off rejection, and endure disappointment. Without drive, there can be no leadership.

HIGH GEAR

Shortly after taking the job as a cabinet salesman, Steve got a call from an old friend who had gotten involved with a network marketing firm based in Ada, Oklahoma. Pre-Paid Legal Services, Inc., was a kind of HMO for the law profession, selling legal service coverage. It seemed like an easy product to sell, and Steve was persuaded to join.

After six months of idleness, Steve now had the equivalent of two full-time jobs. He sold cabinets by day and worked far into the night, every night, on his MLM business. Even breakfasts and lunches became opportunities to hold business meetings. When Steve wasn't on the phone, he was doing business presentations, either in his home or in rented hotel rooms before large groups of people.

"I was working full time and traveling around the state to do meetings," Steve recalls.

It is drive that gives MLM leaders their seemingly superhuman ability to overcome obstacles, slough off rejection, and endure disappointment.

"I'd drive two or three hours to a meeting sometimes, then come home in the wee hours, get up, and go to work the next morning. I had a burning desire to succeed."

LINKS AND ANCHORS

In his prospecting, Steve looked for people who had a similar fire in their bellies. His best prospects often proved to be people with an urgent need for something—a bigger house, a new car, college tuition for their kids—but not enough money to pay for it. These were the people with drive. Steve knew he could count on them to invest the time and effort required to build the business.

He called them "anchors," because they were the leaders, the stabilizers who kept his business from going adrift. Steve's less ambitious recruits he called "links," because they were the ordinary chain links that kept the anchors in place. Often, Steve discovered, it was by following the links that you got to the anchor. Some of his best leaders turned out to be people whom he had not recruited himself, but who had been recruited by his other recruits.

CRITICAL MASS

In those days, Steve's life was a whirlwind of activity. He knew that his downline was growing, that his sales were rising, and that more and more anchors were being added to his organization. But, in the blur of daily work, Steve had no way of knowing how quickly his organization was approaching critical mass.

The Magic Moment took him completely by surprise when it came. That was the day, described in chapter 1, when Steve was going over his account books and suddenly realized that he was making over $1,000 a week in passive, residual income. It had taken six months to reach that point.

"A feeling came over me that was almost spiritual," says Steve. "I could feel it through my whole body. A sense of relief. I saw the light at the end of the tunnel." For Steve, it meant that he could finally quit his day job. He could devote himself full time to his MLM business and become his own boss, once again. "There was this feeling that we'd made up for lost time," says Steve.

AN ENGINE THAT NEVER STOPS

Like all great leaders, Abraham Lincoln had tremendous drive. His poor, troubled background left him with the feeling that he had something to prove. Raised in a log cabin with seven other people, Lincoln lost his mother at age nine and hated his illiterate father. He educated himself and worked as a shopkeeper, postmaster, surveyor, and lawyer, before finally settling on politics. Many of Lincoln's endeavors proved to be dismal failures, but that never quenched the fire of ambition that burned inside him.

Lincoln was always "planning ahead," his law partner William Herndon recalled. His ambition "was a little engine that knew no rest." And so it was with Steve Petroff. Even after he and Nancy began earning combined annual commissions of $1.4 million with Pre-Paid Legal Services, Steve kept on planning and dreaming.

At age fifty-two, he formed Liberty Legal, his own network marketing firm, selling his own brand of legal service coverage. It remains to be seen how Steve's latest gamble will pay off. But one thing is certain. The flames of ambition that were lit inside him all those years ago when his cabinet business failed are still burning strong. That is the kind of drive that makes a leader.

CHAPTER 8

Trait Number 2— Persistence

You become a champion by fighting one more round. When things are tough, you fight one more round," said "Gentleman Jim" Corbett, heavyweight boxing champion of the world from 1892 to 1897.

Corbett was not a particularly strong puncher. He won by staying in the ring. Corbett would dodge his adversary's blows, then strike back with quick jabs, wearing him down by slow degrees. Corbett's "scientific" style of fighting became the standard for modern boxers. He proved that steady, persistent effort could win over brute force every time.

Great leaders, in every field, have known this secret since time immemorial. Staying in the fight is the key to victory. Those who fight on, and never give up, will eventually win, no matter how strong the forces arrayed against them. "Nothing in the world can take the place of persistence," said Calvin Coolidge. "Talent will not; nothing is more common than unsuccessful men with talent. Genius will not; unrewarded genius is almost a proverb. Education will not; the world is full of educated derelicts. Persistence and determination alone are omnipotent."

WASHINGTON'S RETREAT

The trait of persistence has special importance for leaders. It sets an example that others will follow. George Washington demonstrated this principle when he crossed the Delaware and attacked Trenton, New Jersey, in 1776.

Until then, Washington had lost one battle after another. The British had driven him out of New York, then chased him south through New Jersey. Washington's troops were exhausted and starving. Many wore rags on their feet instead of boots. But they had to keep running. A vastly superior British force was right behind them. Washington managed to escape across the Delaware River only by the skin of his teeth.

Defeat seemed inevitable. The retreat from New York had broken the spirit of Washington's army. Winter had set in. Many soldiers were deserting, while others counted the days until December 31, when their enlistment ran out. The Continental Army was disintegrating before Washington's eyes. Meanwhile, across the river, the British were massing for a final assault. Surrender seemed Washington's only option.

> Staying in the fight is the key to victory. Those who fight on, and never give up, will eventually win, no matter how strong the forces arrayed against them.

LEAD BY EXAMPLE

"Most people give up just when they're about to achieve success," said H. Ross Perot. "They quit on the one-yard line. They give up at the last minute of the game, one foot from a winning touchdown."

Washington was no quitter. At a moment when other men would have surrendered, he did just the opposite. He attacked. Crossing the Delaware in the dead of night, he surprised King George's Hessian mercenaries, winning a great victory. Washington's example of perseverance inspired many of his men to sign on for an extra six weeks of service. He used that time to attack the British at Princeton, winning a second victory only days after the first.

The war was far from over. Hard times lay ahead. But never again did the Continental Army come so close to falling apart. The example Washington set at Trenton inspired his men to stick with him through seven more years of war, including the terrible winter at Valley Forge. Persistence proved decisive in America's victory. It was not by superior force that America beat the British, but by hanging on until they were tired of fighting.

A Tale of Endurance

What worked for Washington works for network marketers too. Like all successful networkers, Ken Porter—who now represents a company called Usana—has had his ups and downs in the industry. He has worked with good companies and bad. He has had lean times as well as prosperous ones.

Faced with some of the obstacles Ken encountered, most people would have quit. They would have given up on network marketing, perhaps even concluding that the industry was a scam. But Ken learned early in his sales career that obstacles and difficulties are not unique to MLM. They are part and parcel of any sales career. Ken's first brush with professional selling impressed that lesson indelibly into his mind. "It was a pivotal experience," he recalls. "It defined my life."

The Pledge

While in college, Ken decided to make money one summer by responding to an ad for traveling salesmen. The company was not an MLM firm. It used a traditional door-to-door selling approach. Salesmen were assigned to different areas around the country, where they were expected to knock on doors and sell a line of children's books and audiotapes, featuring Bible stories and other inspirational themes.

When he first signed up for the opportunity, Ken was herded into a huge auditorium with hundreds of other recruits to hear a pep talk from Denis Waitley, a famous motivational speaker. Waitley's speech centered on the theme of persistence.

"Whether you make money or not, this can be the best growing experience of your lives," Waitley promised. He asked each recruit to take a pledge that he would work through the summer, regardless of whether he made money, and never quit until his allotted time was up. Those who were willing to take the pledge were asked to stand up. "Everyone in the room stood up," Ken remembers. But by the end of the summer, most had broken their pledge.

A TOUGH MARKET

Ken was assigned to the Dallas area, along with 120 other recruits. The deal was that they were completely on their own. Each salesman had to pay for his own travel and find his own lodging, at his own expense. Each had to pay for his own inventory up front. The company risked nothing. Ken ended up shelling out $4,000 that summer for food, travel, lodging and inventory. His only hope lay in selling books and tapes, and lots of them.

But the market was tough. The company had assigned Ken to an area—much of it affluent—where people guarded their privacy and did not respond well to strangers knocking on their doors. Most were polite, but they showed little interest in Ken's product.

"No one wanted to let us in," says Ken. "So we had an idea. As soon as someone answered the doorbell, we would grab a book and stick it in their hands. When you hand someone something, their natural tendency is to grab it. It would catch them off guard." Ken would then quickly invite the bemused prospect to hang onto the book overnight and take a look at it. "I'll be back tomorrow," he would say.

ON THE EDGE

For two and a half months, Ken worked his territory diligently, handing out 40 to 50 books per day. But sales were dismal. At one point, Ken had about 200 books out, representing a $3,000 investment for him, which he had put on his credit card.

Ken had worked one particular upscale neighborhood very aggressively. He had saturated the neighborhood with books. But when Ken arrived the next day to do follow-up calls, he was in for a cruel disappointment. Almost every one of the books he had left was sitting outside on the front porch. Some had polite notes attached. Others did not. But not one single person in that neighborhood had agreed to buy the book.

"This is a stinking waste of time," Ken said to himself bitterly. "It's the most ridiculous, dumbest thing I've ever done. Why am I even out here? Why am I trying to push these books down their throats?" Most of the original 120 salesmen in the Dallas area had already quit by that time. Standing there under the hot Texas sun, Ken found himself wondering whether it was they—not he—who had been the smart ones.

A NEW COMMITMENT

But as he stood there, Ken thought back on what Denis Waitley had said at the beginning of the summer: "This can be the best growing experience of your lives." Ken remembered the clapping and cheering. He remembered the resolve that had steeled his heart as he stood and made his pledge.

Looking around at the silent houses, Ken came to grips with his true purpose. "I'm not here for them," he realized. "I'm here for me." And he set his mind once more that he would stick it through to the end. Ken turned out to be one of only three people in the group who kept that commitment.

A SURPRISING DECISION

By the time the summer ended, Ken tallied up his net losses at $2,000. The adventure had been a disaster for him financially. But, just as Waitley had predicted, Ken had learned something about himself that he would never forget. He had learned that he had what it took to overcome obstacles, to keep his commitments and to see a task through to completion.

The following summer, Ken did an amazing thing. He signed on with the very same company, to do the very same job. "There were people in that company who had been succeeding for three to four years, and making tremendous money," says Ken. "I told myself, 'If they can do it, doggone it, I can do it, too.'"

LIFELONG IMPACT

Things went differently this time. Ken ended the summer with close to $20,000 in profit. There were many reasons for his turnaround. The product mix was a bit different this time. He had been sent to a different market, in California, where people seemed more receptive. And Ken's own skill level had grown. But the crucial factor was that Ken had stayed in the fight. Had he not shown up for the second round, the other factors would never have had a chance to kick in.

Only three people from Ken's original group finished out that first summer. He stayed in touch with them in later years. All three went on to achieve great success, in various fields. Just as Waitley had promised, the lesson in persistence that they had learned that summer stayed with them their entire lives. Ken believes it has been the decisive force in his success as a network marketing leader.

A DRIFTER

Lack of persistence, likewise, has been a decisive force in many failures. Soon after joining his first MLM company,

Ken recruited one of his best friends, a man whom we will call "Dave" (not his real name). Dave was something of a drifter. He had earned a bachelor's degree from college, but had not managed to stick to anything since. Dave had worked all sorts of jobs, from repairing broken windshields and doing insurance inspections to managing a car wash and selling cell phones. But nothing seemed to work out. Dave was unhappy everywhere he went. He generally moved on to something else within six to eight months.

Ken hoped that he could rescue Dave from his plight by bringing him into the MLM business. But the same character traits that sabotaged Dave in his other businesses caused him to fail at MLM. "He just wouldn't go out and do it," Ken remembers. "Dave would do everything but talk to people. He would attend conventions, read books. But he wouldn't go out and talk to prospects."

SOMETHING FOR NOTHING

Instead, Dave would keep coming back to Ken, begging for help. And, out of friendship, Ken would give it to him. "I sponsored him into each different company that I joined. I would build his legs for him, sponsoring people below him." In Ken's mind, he was just giving Dave a jump-start. But Dave's engine never seemed to turn over. He just kept coming back for more and more help.

Ken lost track of the number of evenings he spent with Dave, exhorting, coaching and encouraging him. "I felt drained," he says. "We just kept going over the same stuff over and over. It got to where I'd get depressed every time he was coming over."

At one point, Ken knocked himself out building an entire leg of Dave's organization. "He didn't do anything," Ken remembers. "That leg was built 100 percent by my efforts." Instead of picking up the ball and running with it, Dave came to see Ken one night, to ask a favor. Would Ken mind building *another* leg for him?

That was too much for Ken. "I realized that what Dave really wanted was a something-for-nothing paycheck," he says. As nicely as he could, Ken told his friend that he needed to find another way to make a living. Network marketing was just not for him.

Dave is still out there, drifting from one job to the next. Ken, on the other hand, has reached around $400,000 in annual commissions, at this writing. Neither talent nor education separates the two men. But persistence does. Ken learned early to commit to a task and do it. Dave, unfortunately, did not.

FIGHTING THROUGH HARDSHIP

Tom and Bethany Alkazin also know the value of sticking to a task. In their network marketing business, they managed to lead their troops to victory through the sheer force of persistence. Their example of tireless effort inspired their downline to endure months of hardship, hanging on until success was finally within their grasp.

Tom and Bethany were career network marketers. They had spent twenty years in the business and were now full-time MLM leaders, earning about $15,000 per month with a successful nutritional products company. But then disaster struck. The company went bankrupt. Only eight days before Christmas, the company announced that it would cease issuing commission checks. "It was a bleak Christmas that year," Tom remembers. "We had zero income for the next four to six months."

NO DISTRACTIONS

Tom and Bethany adopted a plan that, in some ways, was as risky as Washington's attack on Trenton. Friends of theirs, Ben Boreyko and his brother, Jason, were planning to launch a nutritional company of their own. The Boreykos already had the capital in place. Moreover, Tom and Bethany trusted them to follow through, having known the family for years. The only catch was that it would be months before the new company—called New Vision—would be able to get off the ground. Until then, the Alkazins were on their own.

"We were getting pitched on every deal in town," Tom recalls. Federal Express packages arrived each day from network marketers trying to recruit the Alkazins into other opportunities. But Tom and Bethany believed in the Boreykos and their concept. They refused to be sidetracked.

Contagious Faith

For the first three months, there was no company, no product, no literature, no nothing. "We were selling the dream," says Tom. But most were not buying. Like Washington at the Delaware, the Alkazins watched their army disintegrate. Scores of people from their old downline dropped out. "More than 60 percent of our organization scattered," recalls Tom. "Only a handful bought into the new company."

But the Alkazins were undaunted. After years of networking, they knew that methodical, consistent prospecting would always bear fruit, if they stuck with it long enough. They made a list of all the heavy hitters they knew in the industry, people with a track record for leadership. Then they started calling. Slowly but surely, people began signing on with the new company. "We had a lot of faith, and that's contagious," Tom explains.

The Dark Hours

"What we do not see, what most of us never suspect of existing, is the silent but irresistible power which comes to the rescue of those who fight on in the face of discouragement," wrote Napoleon Hill.

No one fought harder against discouragement than the Alkazins. During the months that they were "selling the dream," they put on a brave front for their prospects. But things were tense at home. Bills went unpaid. The Alkazins were forced to liquidate their life insurance policy and dig deeply into their retirement savings. One day, Tom saw a car coming up the driveway. It turned out to be a man from the bank, checking to see why they had not paid their mortgage in three months. "It was a horrible time," Tom recalls. "We did a lot of praying as a family. There were a lot of tears."

BUILD IN DEPTH

Through that terrible time, Tom and Bethany knew that their single hope lay in working the business, methodically, day by day. That meant prospecting and sponsoring new people into the business. "We had meetings with people, morning, noon, and night," says Tom. "We had one-on-ones with key people, and evening meetings in our home with small groups."

Many of their recruits failed to pan out. Some would join for a while, sponsor a few people, then drop out. But Tom and Bethany did not get discouraged. They knew that attrition was part of the process. In fact, they consciously prepared for it, by going out of their way to establish personal relationships not only with their recruits, but with the people recruited by their recruits, and so on. That way, if the first person quit, they still had the people he left behind. "The trick is to build in depth," Tom explains. "Once you get a person, focus on the people that person is recruiting. That way, you don't rely on any one individual."

THE BREAKTHROUGH

The business grew slowly at first. The Alkazins' first check was for $3,000. Only after a year of hard work did their monthly earnings rise to a consistent $10,000. But, behind the scenes, something was happening. Slowly, invisibly, their efforts were being duplicated by new generations of recruits. Leaders were rising up and training new leaders. "At the one-year mark, we saw that a high level of sponsoring was taking place," says Tom. "There was an excitement in the air. We started getting more attendance at home meetings and at the larger events and rallies. People had caught the wave. You could sense their enthusiasm."

Tom and Bethany's Magic Moment had arrived. Their monthly income began soaring 25 to 50 percent each month. Today, their downline boasts over 100,000 members, with monthly sales exceeding $3 million. Tom and Bethany's personal commissions average more than $50,000 per month.

Consistent Effort

Tom and Bethany attribute their success to "consistent effort." That means working the business methodically, in good times and bad. When times are tough, you don't despair. When times are good, you keep on working.

The days are long gone when the Alkazins struggled to make their mortgage payment. Their palatial 5,000-square-foot home in Carlsbad, California, boasts a guest house, swimming pool, home office building, and basketball court, only a few minutes' drive from the Pacific Ocean. Their three children enjoy four family vacations per year, attend a private Christian school, and have a horse. As New Vision prepares to roll out E-Vision Link—a new division selling Web hosting service—the Alkazins predict even more spectacular growth ahead.

> When times are tough, you don't despair. When times are good, you keep on working.

Yet all their success has not made the Alkazins complacent. They continue working the business, one day at a time, recruiting new leaders and keeping those leaders focused on a single goal. "The most important aspect is sponsoring," says Tom. "How many times per week is someone telling the New Vision story, either by phone or in person? If this number is growing, so is their business." That is the kind of persistence that wins wars. It is also the kind that builds and sustains profitable network marketing organizations.

CHAPTER 9

Trait Number 3— Teachability

In *The Art of the Leader,* William A. Cohen tells the story of the foolish man who looked at the wood-burning stove and said, "Give me heat and then I will give you wood." Of course, the man had it backward. You cannot get heat unless you first supply the wood. That seems obvious to most of us. But, for some reason, we find it harder to accept the same logic when it comes to leadership. Many of us go through life believing that if someone would just give us a break and promote us to a position of responsibility, we would finally be able to demonstrate our leadership ability.

It doesn't happen that way. As Cohen puts it, "If you want to get promoted, you have to be a leader first. Then someone will promote you." Lead first, get promoted later. It seems like a paradox. How can you demonstrate leadership if you don't have followers? The answer is that you must become a follower first. Only when you have mastered the art of following will you be worthy to lead.

A LESSON IN DELEGATION

According to the Book of Exodus, chapter 18, Moses brought the Israelites to Mount Sinai after leading them out of bondage in Egypt. There, he pitched camp and set himself up as judge. All day long, plaintiffs lined up to have Moses settle their disputes. Because there was only one judge and many plaintiffs, the wait was long and tedious.

Then Moses' father-in-law, Jethro, arrived to visit him. The wise old tribal leader sized up the situation. "Why do you alone sit as judge, while all these people stand around you from morning until evening?" he asked Moses. "What you are doing is not good. You and these people who come to you will only wear yourselves out. The work is too heavy for you. You cannot handle it alone."

> Only when you have mastered the art of following will you be worthy to lead.

Jethro then offered some fatherly advice. He told Moses to "select capable men from all the people" and "appoint them as officials over thousands, hundreds, fifties, and tens." These appointees should be assigned to handle the lesser cases, said Jethro. Only the more difficult cases should be brought before Moses. "That will make your load lighter, because they will share it with you," said Jethro. "If you do this and God so commands, you will be able to stand the strain, and all these people will go home satisfied."

YOU MUST FOLLOW BEFORE YOU CAN LEAD

The Bible says that "Moses listened to his father-in-law and did everything he said." He appointed judges and delegated the lesser cases to them. On one level, Jethro's counsel holds valuable lessons for modern corporations afflicted with production bottlenecks and micromanagement. But more remarkable than the sagacity of Jethro's advice is the readiness with which Moses accepted it.

Keep in mind that Moses had been a prince of Egypt, the adopted son of the pharaoh's daughter. He had led the

Egyptian army to victory against the Ethiopians, according to the Jewish historian Josephus. Later, as God's messenger, Moses brought Egypt to its knees, freed the Hebrews, and became ruler of the Israelite nation.

Such a powerful man might have been tempted to laugh off the advice of a desert chieftain such as Jethro. But Moses was too seasoned a leader to scorn good advice. Like all great leaders, Moses had learned to be a good follower first. Even at the height of his power, Moses never outgrew his willingness to learn. His teachability had become a cornerstone of his character.

A HUMBLING EXPERIENCE

Margaret Tanaka learned about teachability the hard way. When she first joined Shaklee Corporation as a distributor, Margaret saw herself as a leader, not a follower. She had risen through the ranks to become a producer at a public television station in Chicago. Having achieved that envied position, Margaret felt she could tackle just about anything in life. But she was wrong. When it came to network marketing, Margaret's professional training and experience proved of little value.

For personal reasons, Margaret and her husband decided to leave the big city and move to Wisconsin. Margaret signed on as a Shaklee distributor just before leaving town. She tried building the business in Wisconsin but soon discovered that she did not take rejection well. "I was very excited at first and told everybody about this great new business I had started," recalls Margaret. But most of her prospects did not share Margaret's enthusiasm. Some questioned the efficacy of the nutritional products Margaret was selling. Others told her that network marketing was a pyramid scheme. "After a month of that, my enthusiasm just disappeared and I became afraid," says Margaret. "I couldn't take the rejection and criticism. For the next three and a half years, I did nothing with the business."

WORKING-MOTHER BLUES

Margaret had been humbled. But she had not yet become teachable. It never occurred to Margaret that there was another way to work the Shaklee business than the way she had tried. Because her method didn't work, Margaret decided that Shaklee itself did not work for her. So she allowed her business to languish for three and a half years.

Events soon conspired to change Margaret's attitude, though. She had taken a community service job in Wisconsin. But after her son was born, she wanted out. Margaret hated leaving her son in day care. Cutting her workweek down to three days only created more stress. "I was still doing a full-time job but getting paid part time," says Margaret. "It was difficult to balance it all. I was miserable."

OPPORTUNITY IN DISGUISE

"Each problem has hidden in it an opportunity so powerful that it literally dwarfs the problem," said Joseph Sugarman, direct marketing guru and chairman of JS & A Group, Inc. "The greatest success stories were created by people who recognized a problem and turned it into an opportunity." So it was with Margaret Tanaka. Being separated from her infant son was a daily heartbreak for her. She could see no way out of her time trap. But Margaret's desperation forced her to reexamine her approach to the Shaklee business. And once she did that, she had taken the first step toward MLM leadership.

Margaret had been recruited in Chicago by a woman named Barbara Lagoni, whom she'd met at a church retreat. From the beginning, Barbara had expressed great hopes for Margaret's future in the business. "She kept in touch with me during the three and a half years that I did nothing, through letters and phone calls," says Margaret. "She kept saying, 'Margaret, you're going to be the leader of Madison, Wisconsin.' But I wouldn't even listen to her. I loved the company, products, and philosophy, but I just didn't believe it was possible." Now it occurred to Margaret that she had never really given Barbara a chance. As a successful leader in Shaklee, Barbara just might have something to teach her.

LEAD WITH THE BUSINESS

"Barbara, I'm ready," Margaret told her sponsor over the phone. "I want you to help me make a plan." Margaret made the three-hour drive to Chicago and sat down with Barbara at her kitchen table. There, her sponsor unveiled to Margaret the simple but powerful principles that would transform her into a leader.

The first was selectivity. Margaret needed to target those prospects who seemed to have leadership potential. "We made a list of all the people I knew," Margaret recalls, "and then went through the list to pick out the people who I thought would make the best partners. Barbara taught me to identify these people and focus on them."

> In order to identify potential business builders, you had to sell the business first and see who was interested.

The second principle was leading with the business. In her sales presentations, Margaret had always tended to lead with the product. She tried to sell her prospects on the health benefits of Shaklee's line of supplements. That was fine for recruiting retail customers and wholesale buyers—people who aspired to nothing more than selling enough product at retail each month to cover the expense of their personal product purchases—but it was no way to find leaders. In order to identify potential business builders, you had to sell the business first and see who was interested. Margaret learned to make the financial benefits of Shaklee's multilevel business opportunity the principle focus of her sales presentation. "I found it was easier for me to sell the business, because that's what turned me on," says Margaret. "For me, Shaklee represented a way for me to work at home so I could be with my baby. I went out to find other moms who were trying to do the same."

METANOIA

The ancient Greeks used the word *metanoia*—from *meta* (above, beyond) and *nous* (mind)—to describe a profound shift in attitude or perspective. Early Christians used it when speaking of repentance and the acceptance of Christ. Today, it has become an important buzzword in managerial science.

In his book *The Fifth Discipline,* MIT management expert Peter Senge applies the word *metanoia* to the profound learning experience that corporations must undergo if they are to succeed. "To grasp the meaning of '*metanoia*' is to grasp the deeper meaning of 'learning' . . ." writes Senge. "At the heart of a learning organization is a shift of mind—from seeing ourselves as separate from the world to connected to the world, from seeing problems as caused by someone or something 'out there' to seeing how our own actions create the problems we experience. A learning organization is a place where people are continually discovering how they create their reality. And how they can change it."

WHAT YOU THINK ABOUT, YOU BRING ABOUT

Margaret, too, had to learn that she was in control of her own destiny. By listening to her sponsor's advice and putting it into effect, she began to experience precisely the sort of paradigm shift that Senge calls *metanoia*. "I realized that I had the power within my own mind to change," says Margaret. "And when I changed my thinking, my business changed. My business grew in direct proportion to me growing on the inside."

Before, Margaret's lack of confidence had caused her to avoid the best prospects. "I would think to myself, 'Oh, that person's not going to be interested,'" she recalls. But now

Margaret had a prospecting list that prioritized the best people. This forced her to overcome her inhibitions and make the approach. Margaret's style of presentation also changed. Before, she had unconsciously conveyed a negative attitude to her prospects. "I was always thinking to myself that it would be difficult to work the business, that I wouldn't be able to find good people, and that people would criticize me," says Margaret. "And so that's exactly what I attracted. What you think about, you bring about. But once I changed my thinking, I found I was attracting a whole different kind of person."

THE SOURCE OF CONFIDENCE

"Confidence doesn't come out of nowhere," said Dallas Cowboy quarterback Roger Staubach. "It's a result of something . . . hours and days and weeks and years of constant work and dedication."

In her previous career as a television producer, Margaret had always been confident and decisive. Yet in network marketing, she had become a timid mouse. Margaret came to realize that her lack of confidence grew directly out of her lack of preparedness. In the television business, Margaret had worked her way up from intern to assistant producer to associate producer. "When I produced my first show, I was confident because I had the training and practice that I had built over time."

Now Margaret would have to repeat that process in MLM. "I realized that I needed to study, to become a student of network marketing." She bought and read every book and publication she could find on the subject. She also read books on personal development and started doing affirmations, visualizing her goals, and monitoring her "self-talk," to ensure that she was keeping a positive attitude. But, most important, Margaret listened closely to her sponsor and put her advice into practice. To Margaret's delight, the rewards came more quickly in her Shaklee business than they ever had in television. Only two months after meeting with Barbara, Margaret attained the supervisor level, the first tier of sales leadership in the Shaklee organization. "That had always been my goal," says Margaret. "But in three and a half years I had never been able to get there."

A TWIST OF FATE

Margaret's business grew quickly. Six months after meeting with Barbara, she was making enough to quit her job. Four years later, her monthly checks were running about $5,000 on average. It seemed that Margaret had achieved her dream. But fate dealt her a cruel blow. Margaret's world was shattered one day when her husband, Richard, died suddenly from an asthma attack.

"It was completely unexpected," says Margaret. "We never saw it coming. I was thirty-four years old, with a five-year-old boy, and my whole life just turned upside-down." The blow was both emotional and financial. Margaret had lost not only a mate, but a provider. As a freelance television technician, Richard had earned linear income, being paid by the hour. The moment he died, his income ceased. Such practical issues were hard for Margaret to think about at the time. She took little interest in working on her Shaklee business for the next few months. Instead, she spent time with her son, taking long trips to the mountains and seashore. "I went to places that would help me heal," she says.

GUARDIAN ANGEL

In any other business, such neglect would have had disastrous consequences. But like a guardian angel, Margaret's downline moved silently to take up the slack for her. Years of hard work had built a deep organization, well-stocked with leaders. Now those leaders rose to the challenge. They began quietly taking over training meetings that Margaret would have led herself in the past. They stepped up their prospecting activity. "The month after my husband died, my monthly check hit $6,500, the largest it had ever been," Margaret recalls. "My income was at a size where it not only met my needs but exceeded them. And it kept on growing. That's when I realized the power of leverage and the power of exponential growth. That can only happen in multilevel."

THE FRUITS OF LEADERSHIP

Margaret's business provided more than financial support during her time of trouble. Word of her loss spread through the network like wildfire. "I got cards and letters from hundreds of people whom I had never even met," says Margaret. "People who were crossline to me and had no financial interest in my business reached out to help me with my group, to run meetings and other things."

As Margaret pored, teary-eyed, through those mountains of cards from well-wishers, she came to realize that the fruits of leadership cannot be measured in money. They are measured in the currency of the human soul. "Real learning gets to the heart of what it means to be human," writes Peter Senge, in *The Fifth Discipline*. "Through learning we recreate ourselves. Through learning we become able to do something we never were able to do. Through learning we re-perceive the world and our relationship to it."

Margaret Tanaka lives in a new world today, a world of constant learning. She is back in the saddle now, building her business and teaching others the secrets of success. But no matter how accomplished Margaret grows in her business or how confident she becomes in her skills, Margaret will never forget that a true leader always has something more to learn.

10

Trait Number 4— Thick Skin

It was a beautiful day on Australia's Sunshine Coast. As Gary Wells sat at his table on the dock, he could hear the screeching of gulls and the waves lapping against the boats in the marina. The outdoor restaurant seemed an unusual setting for a business meeting. But it was not at all unusual for Gary Wells. In recent months, he had grown accustomed to doing business in the most pleasant and exotic of locales. "The great thing about this business," Gary told the Australian man sitting next to him, "is that I get to travel all over the world, write it off for taxes, and make money doing it."

The man looked at Gary oddly. "But if you're traveling all over the world," he said, "how do you manage to work your business at the same time?"

Gary laughed. "This is my business. Sitting here and talking to you, sharing information, telling you about my company. This is the hardest work I do." The men at the table digested this in silence. All were recruits for Life Plus, a Batesville, Arkansas, MLM company that sold nutritional supplements. Gary was the first upline leader they had met from the States. It was clear from their faces that they admired him. In Gary, they saw an ideal of success to which each of them aspired.

The Lonely Path

Gary was still sufficiently new to the world of success that he found it strange to be viewed as a role model. Yet he had clearly earned the title. With a five-figure monthly income, Gary lived like a king in a 4,000-square-foot home in Missouri, surrounded by woods, overlooking a thirty-acre lake. In any given month, Gary's business was likely to take him to Europe, Hawaii, New Zealand, or another captivating destination.

Things had not always gone so smoothly for Gary. Only three years earlier, he had been struggling to build a business from nothing. All the odds had been against him. Even his fiancée had told him he would fail. Like all true leaders, Gary learned to draw on his inner strength. He closed his ears to the naysayers, steeled his heart against his fiancée's gibes, and resolved that he would walk the path of success, even if he had to walk it alone.

Thick Face, Black Heart

Without knowing it, Gary was drawing on a hidden wellspring of energy long known to the sages of ancient China. He had achieved the serene but implacable state of mind that, for centuries, has enabled samurai swordsmen and Kung-Fu fighters to prevail against their foes. Corporate trainer and consultant Chin-Ning Chu has written about this mindset in her book *Thick Face, Black Heart.*

"Thick Face, Black Heart is the secret law of nature which governs successful behavior in every aspect of life," writes Chu, who is president of Strategic Learning Institute in Antioch, California. A practitioner of Thick Face, Black Heart focuses completely on his goal, closing his mind to all other considerations.

According to Chu, most Asians are acutely fearful of losing face or of being humiliated in the eyes of others. But a person with a "thick face" cares nothing for others' opinions. Similarly, people with "black hearts" will pursue their goals with ruthlessness, closing their minds to the pain and turmoil involved in getting there. "Thick Face and Black Heart are two sides of the same coin," writes Chu. To be ruthless, you must have a thick face. To be thick-faced, you must be ruthless.

A LESSON IN RUTHLESSNESS

In the 1980s, American businessmen became enamored of a 2,000-year-old book called *Art of War* by Sun Tzu. Its author was a renowned military strategist of ancient China and a skilled practitioner of Thick Face, Black Heart. Chin-Ning Chu tells the following story about him, in her book *The Asian Mind Game.*

Sun Tzu went to the court of Ho-lu, king of Wu, seeking a position. To test him, the king suggested an experiment. He asked Sun Tzu to train 180 beautiful women—the king's own concubines—as soldiers. Sun Tzu divided the concubines into two military units and appointed the king's two favorite mistresses as captains. After drilling them, Sun Tzu presented his new troops to the king on the parade ground.

Sun Tzu gave his first command. Instead of obeying, the women laughed. Sun Tzu then warned them that there would be serious consequences if they failed to obey. He repeated the command. Once more, the women burst out laughing. Without further warning, Sun Tzu ordered the king's two favorite concubines to be brought forward and beheaded. When they were dead, Sun Tzu gave his order a third time. Not surprisingly, the concubines now performed their drill flawlessly.

THINK ONLY OF CUTTING

In making this demonstration, Sun Tzu acted with ruthless single-mindedness. He showed a complete disregard for others' opinions. The king himself begged Sun Tzu to spare the lives of his favorite mistresses. But Sun Tzu would not listen.

Instead, he focused 100 percent on his goal. Sun Tzu practiced a principle later expressed by the sixteenth-century

Japanese sword master Miyamoto Musashi: "Whatever state of mind you are in, ignore it. Think only of cutting." Though heartbroken by the loss of his favorite concubines, the king of Wu recognized Sun Tzu's merit and made him a general.

GOOD AND EVIL

Obviously, a philosophy such as Thick Face, Black Heart can be used for great evil. But, as Chu explains, it is just as effective in the pursuit of good. "A spear is a useful tool for peacekeeping as well as a weapon of death," she writes. "Thick Face, Black Heart, like the spear, does not in itself contain evil . . ."

As an example, she points to surgeons in the days before anesthetics. The patient would be held down, screaming in agony, while the surgeon cut. It took a Thick Face and a Black Heart to do such work. But it saved lives. Abraham Lincoln was judged a ruthless man for sending thousands of Americans to their deaths. Newspaper editorials of both the North and the South attacked him as a tyrant and butcher. Yet he saved the Union. Even Jesus scandalized Jerusalem when he stormed through the Temple, driving out the merchants and money changers. But today he is called the Prince of Peace.

PLAYING THE FOOL

The master of Thick Face, Black Heart shows his disregard for others' opinions not only through the harshness of his actions, but sometimes through their silliness. He is not afraid to play the fool. Chu relates an ancient Chinese tale about the Kung-Fu fighter Han Xin. Two ruffians stopped Han Xin in the street one day and challenged him to fight. When Han refused, they gave him a choice. If he wouldn't fight, he must crawl like a dog through the legs of the hoodlums' leader. To the amazement and glee of the bullies, Han got down on his hands and knees and crawled.

The news spread all over town. People laughed at Han and called him a coward. Never once did he open his mouth to defend or explain his actions. Most people assumed that he would never amount to anything. But, years later, they were forced to eat their words. Han Xin achieved fame as one of the great warriors of Chinese history. The fact is, he could have killed those bullies with his hands tied. But Han had no reason to fight them. They were not worth the trouble. Secure in his own self-worth, Han felt no need to prove his courage or prowess against such pitiful opponents.

CLOSE YOUR EARS

Success in business depends upon cultivating a self-assurance as indestructible as Han Xin's. No one has ever attained great success without first enduring a withering hail of criticism from friend and foe alike. It takes a thick skin to withstand this sort of assault. But how do you cultivate this quality?

> No one has ever attained great success without first enduring a withering hail of criticism from friend and foe alike.

The best method is to simply close your ears to the critics. After enduring four years of savage attacks from the press, Abraham Lincoln remarked, in his last public speech, "As a general rule, I abstain from reading the reports of attacks upon myself, wishing not to be provoked by that to which I cannot properly offer an answer."

YOUR CRITICS DO NOT SHARE YOUR GOALS

Remember that the naysayers are not on your team. Often, they seek an outcome that is just the opposite of yours. If you listen to them, you will end up achieving their objective instead of yours.

Certainly, this would have been the case had Lincoln heeded his critics. With every setback on the battlefield, the cry went out from press and politicians alike to make peace. But their version of peace meant granting independence to the rebel states. Lincoln's goal was to save the Union, not to destroy it. So he turned a deaf ear to his critics' advice.

EYE ON THE PRIZE

Like Lincoln, Gary Wells kept his eye on the prize. At age forty-four, he was about to retire from the army. The prospect filled him with fear. Gary knew that his pension would pay only 50 percent of his army salary. His skills as a communications security specialist would be of little use in the civilian job market.

"I'd seen a lot of guys leave the army and take jobs for less money than they were really worth," says Gary. "As a chief warrant officer, I'd been the boss for many years. I didn't want to start at the bottom again, punching a time clock and having someone tell me when to take my lunch break or when I could go on vacation."

The only solution was to go into business for himself. Gary explored many options, including franchising, but found the start-up costs too high. At last, he signed up for a real estate course. It did not seem the ideal choice, considering the statistically low earnings of the average real estate agent. But Gary believed that, if he worked hard, he could exceed the average. Real estate seemed to offer his last, best hope for financial freedom.

THE UNKINDEST CUT

Fate intervened in Gary's plans. A friend recommended that Gary try some nutritional products from Life Plus, to help alleviate certain health problems he had developed. Though he warns that similar results cannot be guaranteed for everyone, Gary believes that the products did help him. In fact, he was so impressed by the results that he decided to go out on a limb. Only nine months before his retirement, Gary quit his real estate course and became a Life Plus distributor.

His fiancée, Rebecca, went ballistic. She told him he was being played for a sucker and that the health benefits he had obtained from the products were all in his head. As for network marketing, it was nothing but a pyramid scheme, she said, and Gary was bound to lose his shirt. Rebecca worked as a real estate agent herself. She told Gary that his best hope was to finish his real estate course, get his license, and start selling houses.

NEGATIVE SPOUSE SYNDROME

Of course, Rebecca was only trying to help. In her mind, she wanted to save Gary from pain and disappointment. But her good intentions led her unwittingly to put an obstacle in his path. In later years, Gary came to realize that his experience with Rebecca was common in network marketing. Many of Gary's most promising recruits have dropped out due to pressure from a spouse. "When a husband and wife don't agree about getting involved in network marketing, one of them will eventually win," he says. "You've got two opposing forces, and it's just a question of which one will turn out to be stronger."

> Attrition is high among recruits with negative spouses. Few factors are more destructive to a person's will than twenty-four-hour opposition from a loved one.

In his own recruiting, Gary goes out of his way to speak to negative spouses and try to alleviate their doubts. Often, the problem turns out to be that they have heard secondhand stories about people who lost money in network marketing. This was the case with Rebecca. Winning over such skeptics is a slow process of building trust, explaining the viability of the business, and getting them interested in the products. Helping the positive spouse to earn money as quickly as possible is also key, since his or her success may defuse the negative spouse's objections. But the reality is that these efforts are often wasted. Attrition is high among recruits with negative spouses. Few factors are more destructive to a person's will than twenty-four-hour opposition from a loved one.

THE MISSOURI MULE PRINCIPLE

One of the classic principles of martial arts in Asia is to absorb the force of your opponent's attack and turn it back on him. In *Thick Face, Black Heart,* Chin-Ning Chu observes that many successful people outside the Asian tradition have also discovered the same principle. She points to star running back Jim Brown, who once told an interviewer, "A lot of times when people try to hurt me, it just makes me stronger. I take in that negative energy, run it through my system, and throw it back at them."

Gary Wells developed a similar strategy for handling opposition, which he attributes partly to his Missouri upbringing. "We've got a lot of mules in Missouri," he says, "and they can be pretty stubborn. When somebody tells me I can't do something, it just makes me try harder." Rebecca's opposition spurred Gary to intensify his efforts.

ACCOMPLISH THE MISSION

As an army officer, Gary had been drilled in the principles of combat leadership. Foremost among them was the commitment to "accomplish the mission" at any cost. Failure was not an option in the army. In the spirit of Thick Face, Black Heart, an officer is expected to pursue his goal relentlessly.

Whenever he felt his faith flagging, Gary would remind himself of his mission. He would count down the remaining weeks to his retirement and remind himself of what would happen should he fail to build an adequate residual income.

In combat, the consequence of failure is defeat and death. In his Life Plus business, Gary knew that failure would mean humiliation, menial employment, and subservience to a boss. "Failure was not an option," Gary remembers. "That's what kept me going."

Priming the Pump

The rewards for Gary's commitment came slowly. He spent a lot of time priming the pump. "My first check was about $14," says Gary. "Then the next month I made $30-something, then it was $70-something. I was putting in a lot of work for less than $100 a month." But by the time he retired, nine months later, Gary's monthly commissions had risen to $4,000. They reached the five-figure mark in another year and a half.

Needless to say, Rebecca's objections had long since faded by that point. One year after Gary's retirement, they were married. Rebecca quit real estate and today works alongside Gary in his Life Plus business. It is hard for Gary to imagine nowadays what his life might have been like had he given in to criticism and discouragement. All that he has, he owes to that implacable inner force called Thick Face, Black Heart. Like the Kung-Fu fighter Han Xin, Gary was not afraid to crawl on his hands and knees. And as with Han Xin, his indestructible sense of self-worth has been thoroughly vindicated.

11

Trait Number 5— Positive Attitude

In March 1796, the world had not yet heard of Napoleon Bonaparte. He was an obscure artillery officer only recently promoted to general. When he arrived at Nice that month to take command of his troops, Napoleon's own generals treated him with contempt. They knew that Napoleon had never led an army in battle and resented the fact that he had become their commander largely through political intrigue.

Even less auspicious was the condition of the troops. Napoleon found his men starving and threadbare. Ordered to attack 70,000 crack Austrian and Sardinian troops with only 30,000 men and an envious, disloyal staff, Napoleon faced almost certain disaster.

A PROMISE FULFILLED

It was then that Napoleon demonstrated the exceptional qualities that would one day make him a legend. He said to his troops: "Soldiers! You are badly fed, almost naked. I am going to lead you into the most fertile plains in the world, where you will find big cities and wealthy provinces. You will win honor, fame, and riches."

Even the most optimistic of Napoleon's men must have received this promise with skepticism. But the brash young general promptly made good on it. He smashed the enemy in a series of eighteen major battles. His original orders had been to create a diversion while the main French force marched on Vienna. But after the main force was defeated, Napoleon took charge and marched on Vienna himself, forcing the Austrians to surrender. He had achieved one of the great victories of French history.

SET A POSITIVE EXAMPLE

Napoleon led by example. His thinking was relentlessly optimistic. Where others saw a ragged army threatened with annihilation, Napoleon saw a chance to win "honor, fame, and riches." Not only did he convey his optimism to his men, but he reinforced it with action. Those who followed Napoleon were rewarded by a string of victories.

The combination of positive thinking and positive action proved irresistibly magnetic. It inspired not only the French troops but the envious staff. The generals who despised Napoleon went on to become marshals in his imperial Grand Army. They found their place in history by following the "wild-haired little runt" who had presumed to lead them.

INSPIRE YOURSELF FIRST

The moral of the story is that people will follow you if you give them hope. But first you must inspire yourself. You cannot encourage others if your own thinking is pessimistic and downbeat. Positive thinking is essential for a leader.

"The speed of the leader is the speed of the team," says Jim Meyer, senior national sales director for Primerica. "If you want your team to be excited, you better make sure you're excited." Jim learned about leadership as an athlete. With no special talent for basketball, Jim started at the bottom of his team. He succeeded by cultivating a positive attitude. Now he is building a different kind of team. Jim has found that the principles of positive leadership that he learned in sports can be applied with equal effectiveness in business.

A BRICK WALL

Jim ultimately became a star player on his high school and college basketball teams. Yet after college he felt a void in his life. Basketball had provided an outlet for his competitive drive. But success proved more elusive in the real world. He was turned down for a number of white-collar jobs. Then Jim's father, a union man, got him a job hoisting newspapers on the loading dock of the *New York Daily News*. The pay was good, but Jim's fellow workers made it clear they didn't like go-getters.

"I tried to work hard and get the job done," says Jim. "But the guys would say, 'Hey, slow down, who are you trying to impress? You're making us look bad.'" His fellow workers would stretch out every job so they could collect time and a half. Jim did as he was told. But he yearned to find an outlet for his energy. He looked for white-collar work but always ran up against the same brick wall. "Every entry-level position offered something like $13,000, and maybe in ten years I'd be making $25,000. I thought that was crazy. I was already getting $18 an hour at the *Daily News*."

> You cannot encourage others if your own thinking is pessimistic and downbeat. Positive thinking is essential for a leader.

"MY GAME WAS PRACTICE"

Then a friend invited Jim to an opportunity meeting for A. L. Williams, a company that sold life insurance through network marketing. Jim was enthused about earning residual income and signed up immediately. But success was slow in coming. He spent many months priming the pump.

"People used to ask me how much money I was making," he remembers. "I hated that question. It used to kill me, because I wasn't making anything."

Others might have gotten discouraged, but Jim fell back on his sports experience. When he first tried out for basketball in high school, Jim lacked the natural ability of other team members. He would sit on the bench through every game. "People would ask me why I bothered with basketball, when I never got in the game," he recalls. "But they didn't understand what my game was. My game was practice."

INNER PEACE

During a game, Jim was at the coach's mercy. All he could do was sit there and wait for his number to be called. But between games, he was his own boss. He could practice and work out as much as he wanted. Jim poured everything he had into his practice sessions. He became a "gym rat:" the first one at the gym and the last one to leave. Whenever possible, he signed up for summer camps to sharpen his skills.

Jim found that the key to inner peace was to stop worrying about when the coach would let him play. He treated his practice sessions as if each one were a varsity game. Jim would compete against himself to see how thoroughly he could master each fundamental skill, such as shooting, passing, and dribbling, and how much he could improve his strength and speed, through exercise and conditioning. When he was deeply absorbed in practice, Jim felt at peace. He had as much fun as the other players did in the heat of a game.

THE TORTOISE AND THE HARE

Of course, he wasn't just doing it for fun. Jim knew that there were long-term benefits to the work he was doing. He slowly but surely began to surpass the other players. "Most people don't keep practicing," says Jim. "Because I kept at it, I started passing other people." He also came to exceed many of his teammates in physical strength. "I was in better shape than anyone else. That meant I could run a little faster at the end of the game. I was always looking for that kind of edge, to make up for what I lacked in natural ability."

It took a long time for Jim's self-improvement program to bear fruit. He was like the plodding tortoise in the fable, who eventually overtook the speedy but complacent hare. "As a sophomore in high school, I was one of two kids who did not make the JV team," Jim recalls. "As a junior I came back and led the varsity in scoring." He was made captain of the team in his senior year. Jim repeated the process in college, starting out as a bench warmer and finishing his senior year as team captain.

IN THE GROOVE

One day, during his junior year of college, Jim's coach suddenly called out his number. Jim leaped from the bench and entered the game. His coach had always advised Jim to take time to warm up when he came off the bench. He was supposed to get the feel of the game by touching and passing the ball a few times, rather than going right in for a score. But the moment Jim hit the court, there was no stopping him. "Right off the bench, I had a steal, went in for a layup, got a rebound, hit a shot," says Jim. "I scored nine points in two or three minutes. My coach was like, 'What the heck is going on with you?'"

Just as he had learned to turn his practice and workout sessions into a game, Jim had also developed mental exercises to relieve the tedium of bench-sitting. Jim would visualize himself in the game while sitting on the bench. He would concentrate so intensely that he would feel as if he were already on the court. So when the coach called his number that day, Jim didn't need any warm-up. "I was already in the game mentally," says Jim. "I had the feel. I was in the groove. I wasn't thinking. It was totally unconscious, totally instinctive. An incredible high."

FLOW

Without realizing it, Jim had tapped into the high-performance state known as "flow." University of Chicago psychologist Mihalyi Csikszentmihalyi (mee-HALL-ee chick-SENT-mee-hi) spent twenty-five years investigating this phenomenon. He discovered that flow can be achieved by anyone who follows the right steps. Jim Meyer had stumbled upon these steps almost by accident.

> Flow is about positive thinking. It is about clearing your mind of distractions and discouragement.

Flow is about positive thinking. It is about clearing your mind of distractions and discouragement. Many sales trainers and motivational gurus urge people to "think positive." But that is easier said than done. People have wasted countless hours and much effort trying to force bad thoughts from their minds through willpower alone. Dr. Csikszentmihalyi discovered an easier and far more natural way of keeping the mind free of spiritual poisons.

ANXIETY AND BOREDOM

Csikszentmihalyi started with a simple question: Why are so many people unhappy? In modern life, we take for granted luxuries that would have aroused the envy of Roman emperors and medieval kings. We have television, central heating, automobiles, electric lighting, Internet surfing, and seemingly endless supplies of exotic and tasty foods. Despite all these advantages, "people often end up feeling that their lives have been wasted, that instead of being filled with happiness their years were spent in anxiety and boredom," writes Csikszentmihalyi in his book *Flow*.

He set out to discover why. For twenty-five years, Csikszentmihalyi studied and interviewed people from all walks of life. He talked to janitors, athletes, surgeons, beggars, mothers, dancers, and college professors, asking each one to describe the happiest moments in his or her life. The results were surprising. Most of us think happiness comes from the enjoyment of leisure and luxury. We imagine that a long stay at a Hawaiian resort, with plenty of food, sex, and downtime on the beach, would satisfy our needs. But Csikszentmihalyi learned that just the opposite is true.

PEAK EXPERIENCE

"The best moments," writes Csikszentmihalyi, "usually occur when a person's body or mind is stretched to its limits in a voluntary effort to accomplish something difficult and worthwhile. . . . Such experiences are not necessarily pleasant at the time they occur. The swimmer's muscles might have ached during his most memorable race, his lungs might have felt like exploding, and he might have been dizzy with fatigue—yet these could have been the best moments of his life."

It is struggle—not relaxation—that makes us happy. When we are utterly absorbed in a difficult but worthwhile task, we achieve a state that Csikszentmihalyi calls flow. We lose track of time. We feel at one with our task. The work seems as natural to us as breathing. In the flow state, people have been known to perform remarkable, even superhuman feats. Composers have written symphonies overnight. Athletes have broken records. Businessmen have closed major deals. Amazingly, this high-performance state can be achieved by virtually anyone who follows the right steps.

THE SIX STEPS TO FLOW

There are six stages on the path to flow. They are:

Step One: Treat Your Task as a Game

Whatever you are trying to accomplish, think of it as a game. There should be definite rules, goals, rewards, and challenges. There must be some way to keep score. When Jim was practicing, he strove to shoot more baskets each day and to lift more weight. He drew encouragement from tracking his daily progress.

Step Two: Set a Goal Larger Than Yourself

Search your heart for the deeper motivations that drive you to succeed. Growing up in a tough section of New Jersey, Jim had seen the pain his parents suffered when his older brothers got mixed up in drugs. "That drove me to want to make my parents proud of me," he says. As a boy, Jim zeroed in on basketball as one means to that end. "I used to watch the older guys play, and I'd envision that one day I'd be on that court, too," says Jim. "I wanted to be part of something. I wanted to be recognized, to be somebody."

Step Three: Focus

Focus is a state of total absorption. All negative and disturbing thoughts disappear. You forget about everything except the task at hand. When Jim started playing basketball, he could not keep up with the other players. In group practices, he became anxious and flustered, gripped by negative thoughts, such as embarrassment and fear of failure. It was impossible for Jim to keep his focus.

But during those long hours when he practiced alone, Jim was able to set his own pace. He felt confident and calm. The goals he set for himself were neither too easy nor too hard. They occupied his mind fully but did not overwhelm it. Negative thoughts evaporated. Jim was too preoccupied to entertain them. His practice hours were spent in a state of quiet absorption, free from worries, doubts, and insecurities.

Step Four: Surrender to the Process

Let go and enjoy the process. Don't worry about achieving a particular objective. The work itself should be your objective.

Step Five: Ecstasy

When you have passed through the previous four steps, ecstasy will follow naturally. An intense feeling of joy and well-being will accompany your work.

Step Six: Peak Productivity

The state of ecstasy releases unimaginable stores of energy. You will be astonished at how much you can accomplish under its influence.

A Happy Cabby

As Csikszentmihalyi noted, the principles of flow can be applied to any task, no matter how humble. I once met a cab driver who applied them to the normally frustrating task of navigating the streets of New York City. Most New York cabbies are grumpy and unpleasant, but this fellow radiated happiness. When I told him where I was going, he thought for a minute and started chattering away in his heavy Russian accent.

"I wonder if we would get there faster if I went up the West Side Highway and across 57th Street, or if I went all the way around by the FDR Drive?" he mused. "I think it will take twenty-five minutes to get there by the West Side Highway and only twenty minutes by the FDR. What do you think?" He checked the time on his watch. All the way to our destination, he rambled cheerfully about the different routes he had discovered to reach various points in the city. He knew exactly how many minutes it took to traverse each route. "I am always trying these little experiments," he explained, with a chuckle. For this cabby, each and every fare was an opportunity to discover a new route and to decrease his time per trip. He was so absorbed in this private little game that he never had time to become ill-tempered.

RETHINKING FAILURE

For Jim Meyer, the key to success was learning to be happy, even in failure. His first six months at A. L. Williams (now known as Primerica, after a 1988 merger) provided ample opportunity for practice. During that time, Jim experienced one failure after another. He was twenty-three years old, with no sales experience. Everyone in the office seemed to be making money except him. Jim was tempted to get discouraged. But instead, he fell back on the strategy that had previously made him successful in sports.

> "You're one phone call away, one appointment away, one guest away from changing your life forever."

He resolved to stop thinking about winning. Instead, he would pour all his energy into daily self-improvement. Instead of being a gym rat, he now became an office rat. Primerica encourages sales leaders to open a retail office once they achieve a certain level of volume. Their downlines can then use the office for sales meetings. Jim began hanging around the office as much as he could, befriending and learning from the more experienced leaders. "My upline was my lifeline, and always encouraged me," says Jim.

ONE PHONE CALL AWAY

Just as he had once practiced the skills of dribbling, passing, and shooting, Jim now worked relentlessly on his prospecting skills. He learned to make phone calls, to offer the services and opportunity, to overcome objections and close. It was difficult at first, but Jim was not discouraged by failure.

He learned from each mistake, resolving to make his next sales call more effective than the last.

"I learned in sports that there's always another game," says Jim. "If we lose tonight, there's another game tomorrow night. Learn from that game and get on with it." Jim also knew that you didn't have to wait for a new game to turn a losing streak into a winning one. "You're always one basket away from a momentum change," he says. "If you're down a couple points, you get a steal, you make a shot, you're back in the game. It's the same in this business. When things aren't going right, you can always start over. Go prospect somebody, go meet with somebody, go follow up on somebody, and keep a good attitude. You're one phone call away, one appointment away, one guest away from changing your life forever."

CONSTANT IMPROVEMENT

In effect, Jim had turned his business into a game. The object of the game was to improve the effectiveness of his sales presentation. It did not matter if the sale fell through. As long as Jim saw a clear improvement in his presentation, he felt like a winner.

The thrill of constant, daily improvement—and the hope it instilled of future success—more than compensated for Jim's temporary lack of income. He knew in his heart that if he kept on practicing, he would one day make the team. "I kept thinking, 'If I can have fun when I'm making no money, imagine what my life will be like when I'm making money.'"

CONTAGIOUS ENTHUSIASM

Jim did not have long to wait. His enthusiasm was contagious. The more deeply absorbed he became in the "game" of self-improvement, the more confidence he showed in his sales presentations. Eventually, Jim's prospects started signing up.

When he signed on with A. L. Williams, Jim's goal had been to make an extra $500 a month, so that he could afford to move out of his parents' house. He had assumed that his MLM business would remain a part-time endeavor. But by his second year in the business, Jim was already earning more money from A. L. Williams than he was from his day job. "My first six months in the business, I made no money," he recalls. "The second year I made $70,000." It took Jim another four years to reach $400,000 and six more to hit $900,000. His annual income finally exceeded a million dollars in 1998. "I wanted to make a million dollars in twelve months before I turned thirty. It took me until thirty-seven. I missed it by seven years. So I guess I'm a failure," Jim laughs.

THE COCOON

Teamwork is key to Jim's success. Like Napoleon at Nice, Jim relies on his troops for victory. In classic Napoleonic fashion, he has learned to energize his army by sharing his optimism with them. Jim does this by building a "cocoon" around his people.

A caterpillar weaves a cocoon to protect itself from predators while it changes into a butterfly. Jim believes that a leader must build a cocoon around his team, as a defense against discouragement and negative thinking. Within that cocoon, a losing team can metamorphose into a winning one. The flow of the leader can become the flow of the team. "We wanted to build a barrier around our team," Jim explains. "We didn't want to allow outside people to influence what we were going to do."

TEAMWORK

Jim started by giving his team a sense of identity. He called them "The Maniacs." To ensure that every new person felt special, Jim and his team leaders issued Maniac baseball caps and T-shirts at all big events.

"We were the youngest team in the company and the craziest," says Jim. "We were the most excited team at every event. We'd give standing ovations for every speaker. Anytime one of our people got recognized, we'd go ballistic. People would shout, 'Here we go, Maniacs, here we go!' It was like a Knicks game."

ALIGNMENT = VELOCITY

Jim kept his team focused by spotting and correcting negative attitudes quickly, before they had time to take root. That way, he kept everyone moving in the same direction. "A sales team is like a car," says Jim. "If your front tires are out of alignment, you can't get any velocity. Alignment equals velocity."

After recruiting meetings, Jim would often take a core group of eight to ten leaders out to a restaurant or diner, where they would talk and "get inside people's heads," as he puts it. People would express their frustrations at these meetings. Perhaps some key person had dropped out of their organization. Perhaps recruiting had been slow that month. Perhaps one of their leaders was depressed and struggling financially and seemed in danger of dropping out. Jim would listen to all these problems. But then he would steer the complainer back to more positive subjects.

STICK TO FUNDAMENTALS

"Whatever people focus on, it grows," says Jim. "When people get stuck on something negative, you have to break their pattern." Jim would downplay the problem and focus on the solution. He might say, "Okay, so this guy on your team is struggling right now, just like you and I were struggling a few years ago. And how did we get out of it?" By prospecting, of course. By getting in the flow. By remembering that you're just one phone call away from changing your life forever. And so on. "Exactly!" Jim would say. "So let's get this guy in here and talk to him about prospecting."

According to Jim, the most important job of an MLM leader is to keep steering people back to the fundamentals. "A lot of times when people start making money, they start thinking that they've got to do things differently," he says.

"They overcomplicate the business. They say, 'Okay, I've got my guys now. Let me train them.' But people don't need that much training. They need to get out and prospect. In our business, you keep doing the same thing over and over again, with more and more new people. If you've got the fundamentals down right, you keep doing it over and over again, and allow your team to continually duplicate itself."

SHARE THE VICTORY

When Napoleon marched against the Austrians and Sardinians in 1796, his optimism spurred the French troops to attack. But their enthusiasm would have faded quickly if things had gone badly on the battlefield. Napoleon's task of inspiring his troops grew easier with each victory. There is no better motivator than success.

In the first months of his business, Jim spent a lot of time "selling the dream." He was on the phone every night, reminding his leaders that "You're only one phone call away from changing your life." But then a strange thing happened. "I started getting phone calls coming the other way," he recalls. "People called to tell me how great things were going. Attendance at their meetings was going up. Their incomes were growing. Instead of me selling them the dream, they were selling the dream back to me."

For Jim, it was the ultimate victory. His quest for success had begun long ago, when he tried to make his parents happy by succeeding in basketball. Now Jim was still striving to make others happy. And his Primerica business gave him a practical way to do it.

"It's biblical," says Jim. "If you give, you're going to receive. I think the reason I've been successful is that I'm driven to help others achieve their goals and dreams."

THE FLOW OF WORK

"Satisfaction lies in the effort, not in the attainment," said Mohandas Gandhi. "Full effort is full victory." Jim Meyer learned this truth firsthand. Through flow, he attained happiness when success was still a distant dream. By the time success caught up with him, Jim was so accustomed to being happy, he hardly even noticed the change.

At a certain point, Jim's upline informed him that he had become a millionaire. His net worth was over a million dollars. Most people would have popped open a bottle of champagne. But Jim felt strangely unmoved by it all. "Sometimes in sports," he says, "team members celebrate so much when they win that it proves they didn't expect to win. I expected it to happen all along. For me, it was just business as usual." Like Napoleon at Nice, Jim Meyer had envisioned "honor, fame, and riches" where the rest of the world saw only futility. His faith had brought victory, for himself and others. But Jim's greatest triumph had nothing to do with money. It occurred within the reaches of his own mind, where despair and frustration transformed into hope, through the subtle magic of flow.

CHAPTER 12

Trait Number 6— Compassion

In the last chapter, we saw how Napoleon's positive attitude energized his troops. But optimism was not the only thing he gave them. When Napoleon saw the pathetic state of his army at Nice, he issued a week's ration of food and liquor. Next, he fired off a sharply worded message to Paris, demanding better supplies for his men. Only after addressing these basic needs did Napoleon finally raise the issue of attacking the Austrians.

We think of Napoleon as a brutal conqueror. And indeed he was. But without the loyalty of his troops, he would have made no conquests. Napoleon won their loyalty by showing his troops that he cared. The Grand Army trusted Napoleon to look out for its welfare. On the night before the Battle of Austerlitz, Napoleon circulated among his troops, reassuring them personally that, if they were wounded on the battlefield, special measures had been taken to get them medical help as quickly as possible. That sort of personal concern built a bond between Napoleon and his men that could not be broken.

THE GREAT TEMPTATION

The temptation is great, for a leader, to think of people as nothing more than tools or instruments of his will. Foolish leaders will drive their people relentlessly, with no thought to their feelings or frailties. Such leaders find it difficult to motivate people. They are always wondering why their people are slow to respond to a challenge and even slower to follow instructions. At worst, such leaders will face outright hatred, rebellion, and disobedience from the ranks.

A true leader, however, will never let his people forget that he puts their interests first. He will do all in his power to make their jobs easier. He will praise people for their successes and blame himself for their failures. He will push people only as hard as they are willing to push themselves. In return, they will give him loyalty. They will work harder for a benevolent leader than they ever would for a despot.

> A true leader, however, will never let his people forget that he puts their interests first.

DRIVEN TO SUCCEED

Cindy Samuelson was driven to succeed. Reared in poverty, she had set her mind, early in life, to become rich and was willing to do almost anything to achieve great wealth. Cindy was barely five years old when her parents brought her to the United States from the Philippines. Her father was an American serviceman, her mother a Filipina. "I had a childlike wonder for this incredible country," she remembers. "I began dreaming of what it would be like to grow up and be wealthy."

But there were roadblocks along the way. Cindy's father was a bitter man, filled with envy and hatred for people better off than himself. "He was very left wing," Cindy remembers. "He hated the wealthy. He hated business. Even as a little girl, I knew something was wrong with his philosophy." Before long, Cindy's father simply abandoned his family. His wife and five children were left to fend for themselves.

A DESPERATE PROMISE

Cindy's mother got a job scrubbing furniture that had been burned in warehouse fires. It was hard work. Her delicate hands became raw, callused, and filled with splinters. Cindy remembers standing with her mother in a welfare line, gazing in sorrow at her mother's ruined hands. "She had her arms around us, all five of her children," says Cindy. "Tears were pouring down her face."

It was then that Cindy's mother whispered a promise to her children. "When you are older," she said, "you will not have to live this way." She told them that if they worked hard, they would never again stand in a welfare line. And, in fact, they never did. Shortly thereafter, Cindy's mother got an assembly-line job at a Motorola plant. Her five children jumped up and down, screaming with joy, when she came home with her first $60 paycheck. "It was the most money we'd ever had," says Cindy.

BY ANY MEANS NECESSARY

Poverty left its mark on Cindy's soul. Her desperation to succeed became an obsession. She grew up to become an aggressive saleswoman, pushing for the close at any cost, with little concern for the needs of her clients. "There was a steeliness in my eyes," she says. "I was made of steel. It scares me. I could easily have become someone like Leona Helmsley—an arrogant, hated person."

Cindy's Machiavellian approach to business finally caught up with her when she pushed her own husband into a disastrous investment. Bob and Cindy Samuelson had built a successful warehouse business. But Cindy wanted more. She pleaded with Bob to invest in a company selling a pool-cleaning chemical. Smelling a loser, Bob refused. But Cindy went ahead and signed the contract without his permission. "I still can't believe I did that," she laments.

A HUMBLING EXPERIENCE

The Samuelsons ended up losing their entire life savings of $500,000. "We liquidated our pension plans, sold our business, and mortgaged our house," says Cindy. "My husband had to go out and get a job for half of what he had earned before. He was so angry at me, it took two years of marriage counseling for us to get through it."

Reality struck home for Cindy when she pulled up to the supermarket check-out counter one day and discovered, to her horror, that there was not enough money in her checking account to pay for her groceries. She felt as if she had been transported back to her impoverished childhood, through some diabolical time warp. "Tears just poured out of my eyes," says Cindy. "I was devastated."

AGGRESSIVE SELLING

Psychologist Abraham Maslow once said, "When your only tool is a hammer, every problem looks like a nail." So it was with Cindy Samuelson. Aggressive selling had always worked for her in the past. Now she returned to the same strategy, with the hope of regaining success.

Cindy was deeply ashamed of what she had done. She wanted desperately to redeem herself in her husband's eyes. That meant replacing the money she had lost. But the only way Cindy knew of accomplishing this was to employ brute force—the same "take-no-prisoners" approach to business that had gotten her into trouble in the first place.

OBSESSION

It worked for a while. Cindy joined a network marketing company and started recruiting. Her business grew rapidly. Cindy bludgeoned people into joining by the sheer force of her personality. She wouldn't take no for an answer. And once people joined, Cindy would ride them mercilessly to go out and recruit more people. "I was a workaholic," she remembers. "I would only sleep two or three hours a night. I was obsessed. And because I drove myself so hard, I expected others to work just as hard."

Cindy's top producer was a woman named Ruth. "She was a housewife with a great sense of humor. She loved people and was just a delight. Everybody was magnetized to her." Over an eighteen-month period, Ruth built a downline that accounted for a large portion of Cindy's income. But for Cindy, it wasn't enough. "I just kept driving her and driving her. I was very demanding and bossy."

CROSSING THE LINE

One day, Cindy pushed too far. She had been pressuring Ruth for days to get in touch with an acquaintance whom Cindy felt was a hot prospect. But Ruth had not done it yet. At an opportunity meeting, just before Cindy was about to mount the podium to speak, she asked Ruth once again whether she had contacted the woman. Ruth said no. "What are you thinking?" Cindy blasted her. "This is a very bright woman and you have access to her. Why haven't you taken care of it yet?"

Ruth looked at her blankly. "Drop f------ dead," she said and walked away. Cindy was stunned. "I couldn't believe she had said that to me, right to my face, right in front of everybody. My first thought was, 'How dare she do this in front of the organization!'" But later, when she had cooled down, Cindy realized that Ruth had been right. "She was the only person in the world who had the courage to stand up to me," says Cindy. "I was devastated, because I realized that she was absolutely right. I could hardly think, I was so shaken up. I spent four months licking my wounds."

THE TURNING POINT

In hindsight, Cindy believes that her confrontation with Ruth marked a turning point. She realized that she needed to change. "I had to learn how not to be a dictator," she says.

"I had to learn how to lead by respect and mutual admiration, instead of by fear and intimidation."

Often in life, we find the teacher we need only when we are ready to hear him. So it was with Cindy Samuelson. One day, she attended a training meeting for her MLM company, in Phoenix, Arizona, where she lives. A successful sales leader named Bob Schmidt had come from out of town to speak. Enthused by his message, Cindy approached Bob after his speech and begged him to teach her. She asked him to spend a day driving around Phoenix with her, on her sales calls, to try to troubleshoot her approach.

> Often in life, we find the teacher we need only when we are ready to hear him.

BOB'S THREE LESSONS

Bob agreed. It wasn't long before Cindy's problem became obvious. "She was so intense that she was pushing people," he later remarked, in *Network Marketing Lifestyles Magazine* (June 1999). "She backed them into a corner." As a result, people were signing up with Cindy just to get her off their backs. Then, after Cindy left, the pressure was off and they forgot all about their commitment. Cindy's downline was a revolving door. She had one of the highest sign-up rates in the company and one of the lowest retention rates.

Bob taught Cindy three things. First, he taught her detachment: to let go of her intense desire to close a sale and just enjoy the process. Second, he taught her nonconfrontational selling: to give people room and respect their space. Finally, he taught her to build in depth: to form relationships with the recruits of her recruits, so that when she lost a frontline person, it would not be the end of the world. How Cindy put these principles to work in her business will be discussed in detail in chapter 17.

BONDS OF LOYALTY

Cindy formed a partnership with Bob that allowed them to build on each other's strengths. Together they built a powerful, multimillion-dollar sales organization with an international reach. But it wasn't all a bed of roses. Their parent company went bankrupt in 1994, due to management problems. In an instant, their income vanished, leaving them high and dry. All their hard work together seemed wasted.

But Cindy still had the most valuable asset of all: the new skills she had built through years of working with Bob. She and Bob joined a new untested company called New Vision International. Using his non-invasive approach, Cindy was able to build her downline quickly, with far less turnover than before. New Vision's sales grew to $200 million in five years, making Cindy a multimillionaire, and bringing prosperity to many in her downline.

TOUGH LOVE

"For the first two and a half years I was in network marketing, my husband didn't offer a word of encouragement," Cindy remembers. But now he believes in the business. Helped by her New Vision revenue, Cindy's husband, Bob, bought four franchises and no longer worries about his retirement. "I can afford to be a stay-at-home mom today," says Cindy.

Proverbs 11:2 states that, "When pride comes, then comes disgrace, but with humility comes wisdom." Cindy attributes all her success to that humbling experience, years ago, when a distributor named Ruth told her to drop dead. "We didn't speak for over a year," Cindy recalls. "But she continued to work her business. I think of her now as someone very precious in my life. You learn so much more from the truth than you do from false applause or false compliments. It was the turning point in my career. I was suffering. And I could never have become as successful as I became in this business, had I not learned that lesson."

CHAPTER 13

Trait Number 7— Vision

In the summer of 401 B.C., ten thousand Greek mercenaries pitched camp outside Babylon. They were exhausted, hungry, and filled with despair. For months, they had marched through endless deserts, foraging desperately for food while they fought one bloody battle after another. None had any real stake in this war. They were soldiers of fortune, fighting for pay. Nonetheless, they had fought bravely for their commander, Cyrus, a Persian prince who was contending with his brother for the throne.

Now Cyrus was dead, killed in battle. There was no more reason to fight. All the Greeks wanted was to go home.

The Greek leaders made a truce with the Persians and went to their camp to negotiate. The Greek mercenaries— whom history remembers as the Ten Thousand—waited anxiously for the return of their envoys. But they waited in vain.

Only a single Greek, horribly wounded, came stumbling back into the camp. With his dying breath, he warned the Ten Thousand that the envoys were dead. The Persians had slaughtered every last member of the peace party and were now coming to finish off the leaderless Greek army.

79

A VISION FROM ZEUS

Panic spread through the camp. Dismayed by the noise of despair and confusion, a young Athenian named Xenophon walked away from the camp, found a quiet place to think, lay down, and promptly fell asleep.

He dreamed that he was back in Greece, looking at his house in the country. Suddenly, a mighty thunderbolt of Zeus crackled from the sky, striking his house. Before Xenophon's wondering eyes, a heavenly light glowed from within the house, burning brighter and brighter as he watched. Thereupon he awoke.

In his book *Anabasis,* Xenophon doesn't explain precisely how or why, but when he awoke from that dream he was utterly convinced that Zeus had appointed him to lead the Ten Thousand out of Persia.

SHARING THE VISION

Xenophon was not even a soldier, but a civilian staffer. Moreover, he was young and without experience in leading men. Yet somehow his dream had given him faith that he was equal to the task.

Xenophon took immediate action. He stood up before the disheartened Greeks and made a speech. Xenophon pointed out that the Persians were little better than slaves. They knew only how to obey. Without a king to command them, they were nothing. But the Greeks were free men. They could think for themselves. If one leader fell, another would rise up to replace him.

"They think we are defeated," cried Xenophon, "because our officers are dead and our good old general Clearchus. But we will show them that they have turned us all into generals. Instead of one Clearchus they have ten thousand Clearchuses against them!"

A COMMON PURPOSE

Xenophon's faith was contagious. Almost instantaneously, the dispirited and confused soldiers were on their feet cheering. Xenophon's speech had given them a common goal and a vision for ultimate victory. That very day, the Ten Thousand set out on one of the most harrowing marches in military history. They couldn't go back to Greece the way they had come because they had already stripped the land bare of food. So they headed north, intending to take a circuitous, 2,000-mile route to the sea. The Persian cavalry dogged them every step of the way. In the mountains of countries that are now Kurdistan, Armenia, and Georgia, fierce tribesmen showered the Greeks with arrows while they shivered and bled in the snow. Through it all, Xenophon urged them on, imbuing them with his unshakable faith that they would succeed.

> The consequences of failure may be less dire in business, but a compelling vision is no less vital for success.

Four months after their nightmare march had begun, the Greeks arrived at a hill. When they climbed to the top of it, they began weeping, cheering, and crying out, "Thalassa! Thalassa! The sea! The sea!" They were free. The coastline marked the end of enemy territory. Across the water lay Greece. Thanks to Xenophon's leadership, they had escaped certain destruction.

"A PICTURE OF THE FUTURE"

"Where there is no vision, the people perish," says Proverbs 24:16. In the case of the Ten Thousand, this warning applied literally. Without Xenophon's vision to pull them together, the Ten Thousand would have disintegrated into a fearful, disorderly rabble. The Persians would have slaughtered them easily.

The consequences of failure may be less dire in business, but a compelling vision is no less vital for success. In *The Fifth Discipline,* MIT management expert Peter Senge defines vision as a "picture of the future we seek to create." He writes: "One is hard-pressed to think of any organization that has sustained some measure of greatness in the absence of goals, values, and missions that become deeply shared throughout the organization. IBM had 'service'; Polaroid had instant photography; Ford had public transportation for the masses; and Apple had computing power for the masses. Though radically different in content and kind, all these organizations managed to bind people together around a common identity and sense of destiny."

PERSONAL VISION VERSUS SHARED VISION

Most network marketing leaders have a vision of one sort or another. It might be a short-term vision, such as, "We're all going to go out and meet fifty people this week and pitch them on the opportunity." Or it might be a long-term vision, such as, "We are going to achieve $5 million in organizational volume." Yet all too often, the personal vision of the leader fails to ignite any spark in his downline.

All businesses, not just MLM, face this challenge. "Many leaders have personal visions that never get translated into shared visions that galvanize an organization," notes Senge. "What has been lacking is a discipline for translating individual vision into shared vision." In an effective organization, vision is more than just an empty mission statement e-mailed to the staff. It is a sense, shared by every team member, of complete identification with the goal or purpose of the organization. Xenophon had the instinctive ability to create such a "shared vision." Those who aspire to MLM leadership must acquire that skill.

THE CIRCLE OF INFLUENCE

How can you, as a leader, tell other people what to think and feel? You can't. And even if you try, they won't necessarily listen to you. To reach the hearts and minds of others, you must start by looking within yourself. In his book *The 7 Habits of Highly Effective People*, Stephen Covey explains why.

He says that one of the key attributes of an effective person is the ability to distinguish between those things that lie within his power to change and those that do not. Think of your world as composed of two circles, the smaller circle inside the larger one. The smaller circle is your Circle of Influence. All those things that you have the power to change lie within that circle. The larger circle represents your Circle of Concern. It contains all those things that you care about but can't really change: the tax rate, the weather, the behavior of your boss, and so on.

Ineffective people spend a lot of time ruminating about their Circle of Concern. But "proactive people focus their efforts in the Circle of Influence," writes Covey. "They work on the things they can do something about." Paradoxically, the more tightly you focus on your Circle of Influence, the larger it grows. Your personal power increases. Soon you discover that you are able to affect people and events that used to lie beyond your control. Your Circle of Influence begins to envelop more and more of your Circle of Concern. It is by this means that a leader shares his vision with other people. Nurture the vision within yourself, and soon it will spread to others.

> To reach the hearts and minds of others, you must start by looking within yourself.

THE POWER TO CHANGE

Sherry Ellingson of Urbandale, Iowa, had a vision. It did not present itself as dramatically as Xenophon's. No thunderbolt from Zeus struck her in the night. But Sherry's vision, like Xenophon's, had the power to change her life and the lives of others.

It came to her one day when Sherry asked her husband for money. "What for?" he responded. It was a reasonable question. Yet in all her married life, Sherry had never had to answer it before. She had always made good money as a saleswoman for Airborne Express and had kept her own bank account. After the birth of her second child, however, Sherry quit her job. The Ellingsons' family income dropped by a third. They cut back on vacations and moved to a cheaper neighborhood. Sherry was willing to make these sacrifices, in exchange for the joy of staying home with her children. But she had not counted on having to ask permission for every little purchase. Sherry found that she didn't like it.

CREATIVE TENSION

Her experience caused her to start daydreaming. Sherry imagined a life in which she did not have to choose between motherhood and financial freedom. In her vision, she could have both. She would have the freedom to spend all day with her children, while still earning a substantial income from a home-based business.

Sherry had taken the first step toward becoming a visionary leader. She had tapped into the power of "creative tension." Peter Senge defines creative tension as "the gap between vision and current reality." It is the difference between where you are and where you want to be. Some people get discouraged when they become aware of that gap. But effective people draw strength from it.

> The first step toward cultivating a personal vision is to realistically acknowledge the gap between vision and reality and embrace it as a force for good.

Senge likens creative tension to a rubber band. The wider the gap between vision and reality, the tighter the rubber band is stretched. Tension builds. And, as Senge explains, there are only two ways to relieve that tension: "Pull reality toward the vision or pull the vision toward reality." You can use that tension to hurl yourself toward your goals, like a slingshot. Or you can allow it to drag you down to despair. The first step toward cultivating a personal vision is to realistically acknowledge the gap between vision and reality and embrace it as a force for good.

THE ROLLER COASTER

Sherry embraced the gap by seeking a vehicle to turn her vision into reality. She chose a network marketing firm called Rexall Showcase, which sold nutritional products. It was a subsidiary of Rexall Sundown, Inc., formed in 1991 when Sundown Vitamins, Inc., acquired the venerable Rexall drugstore trademark.

Sherry did a lot of pump priming. In between the chores and responsibilities of motherhood, Sherry managed to squeeze in about twenty hours of prospecting per week. It was a frustrating process. Sherry went through what she calls a "roller coaster" of emotion, as people joined her downline, then later dropped out. Entire legs of her downline would die off, after Sherry had worked months to build them up. She would have no choice but to go back and start prospecting all over again.

DAILY CLARIFICATION

According to Senge, a visionary leader refuels himself each day. He keeps the rubber band taut, maintaining a high state of creative tension by (1) "continually focusing and refocusing on what [he] truly wants" and by (2) "continually learning how to see current reality more clearly." The visionary leader never forgets his dreams. But he never loses track of how far he still has to go to attain those dreams.

Sherry's business remained sluggish for two and a half years. Many times she felt like quitting. But Sherry would always remind herself of her goals. She would envision herself as a stay-at-home mom with a good residual income. And that vision would keep her going. It also helped her to overcome her doubts about the MLM industry. Selling Airborne Express delivery service had been a breeze compared to network marketing. It was hard trying to convince people to commit to a business opportunity. But Sherry never thought seriously about returning to the corporate world. "The thought of it turned my stomach," she says. "There was no way I was going to rely on somebody else for a paycheck or ask someone's permission for time off to go see my kids play."

AWARENESS OF OBSTACLES

Sherry always kept her dream before her. But, at the same time, she maintained an acute awareness of the obstacles in her path. One thing that bothered Sherry about her business was how much time she had to spend doing things she hated. "If there's one thing I've never enjoyed about network marketing, it's prospecting," says Sherry. "I'm an introvert, when it comes to meeting new people. That's a tough thing to be in this industry."

Traditional methods of prospecting that targeted friends, family, and neighbors were intimidating to Sherry. She focused on the cold market, running classified ads or sending out direct mailings. These impersonal methods reminded Sherry reassuringly of selling in the corporate world. They also shielded her from the emotional trauma of getting rejected by people she knew. Yet Sherry could not help but feel that she was missing out on something. The twenty hours she spent prospecting each week were filled with tedium and anxiety. If she did not enjoy her work, what was the point of doing it? Sherry realized that she was still far from her dream. But the distance between vision and reality only heightened her creative tension.

TRIAL AND ERROR

"When you are immersed in a vision," says Ed Simon, president of Herman Miller, who is quoted in *The Fifth Discipline,* "you know what needs to be done. But you often don't know how to do it. You run an experiment because you think it's going to get you there. It doesn't work. New input. New data. You change direction and run another experiment. Everything is an experiment, but there is no ambiguity at all. It is perfectly clear why you are doing it."

In hindsight, Sherry realizes that her first two and a half years in network marketing were a series of failed experiments. But no matter how far she wandered offtrack, the power of her vision always drew her back. It was through this sort of random experimentation that Sherry accidentally stumbled upon the method that would finally galvanize her downline and lead her to success.

FOLLOW YOUR HEART

Sherry found that she liked the Internet. At first, she saw no connection between it and her MLM business. To her, the Internet was a place where she could get travel and medical information or network with other working mothers through message boards and chat rooms. But Sherry soon discovered that many of the people she met online turned out to be good prospects for her Rexall business.

Sherry developed a system for online prospecting. She would go into chat rooms or message boards—especially those related to health, nutrition, or working at home—and strike up dialogues with people. If the subject was health, she would steer the discussion to Rexall products. An even better opener was to ask people what they did for a living. Generally, they would ask her the same question back, giving Sherry the perfect excuse to tell them about her MLM business. Once she had their interest, Sherry would move the relationship to the next step. When she first started out, Sherry would ask for prospects' addresses, so she could send them an audiotape. Later, she put up a Web site and simply directed prospects to the Web address, where they could obtain all the information they needed on Rexall and even sign up online.

ENROLLMENT VERSUS COMPLIANCE

Online prospecting was just what Sherry needed. It enabled her to reach large numbers of people, without face-to-face selling. Sherry realized that if it could work for her, it could work for others. She was not the only person who disliked conventional prospecting. But Sherry could not just order her downline to adopt the new method. Like all leaders, she had to win people over to her vision.

Peter Senge calls this the "enrollment" process. Enrollment means joining something by choice. It is the opposite of "compliance," which means going along with something because you have to. Factory workers might show up faithfully five days a week, out of compliance with company rules. But if you want them to double their productivity, you'll probably have to get their voluntary enrollment in the plan.

THREE GUIDELINES FOR ENROLLMENT

According to Senge, there are three things a leader can do to encourage enrollment:

1. **Be enrolled yourself. Lead the way by demonstrating enthusiasm for your vision.**
2. **Be on the level. Don't insult people's intelligence with pie-in-the-sky promises and projections. Present the problems and obstacles honestly.**
3. **Let the other person choose. Make your case and then go about your business. Don't beg, pester, nag, browbeat, or manipulate people into following you. Make sure your people know that they are free to decide for themselves.**

"The hardest lesson for many managers to face," writes Senge, "is that, ultimately, there is nothing you can do to get another person to enroll or commit. . . . The guidelines above simply establish conditions most favorable to enrollment, but they do not cause enrollment."

SOLDIERS AND CIVILIANS

When William A. Cohen left the air force and entered a civilian management job, the president of his company gave Cohen a lecture. "Now, Bill," said the president, "I know that you have led military organizations, but it's not the same thing leading civilians. You can't just give an order and see it carried out."

Cohen listened patiently, but he realized that his boss had a few misconceptions about how the military worked. A commander who simply barks out orders will seldom get real obedience. In his book *The American Army in France,* World War I General Harbord wrote that every time an order is given to move forward in battle, the men take an "inarticulate vote" before obeying. "The Army does not move forward until the motion has been carried," wrote Harbord. "'Unanimous consent' only follows cooperation between the individual men in ranks."

AN UNPOPULAR ORDER

In *The Art of the Leader,* Cohen describes how one combat commander persuaded his men to follow a distinctly unpopular order. He was Colonel Pappy Boyington, commander of the famous Black Sheep fighter squadron in World War II. His pilots were all "black sheep," rejects from other units, yet they shot down more Japanese planes than any other squadron.

After a long, hard tour of duty, the Black Sheep were ordered to the rear for a much-needed rest. The night before they shipped out, the entire squadron got drunk. Then Colonel Boyington got a radio message: "Essential that you bomb targets in Rabaul tonight." He went to the quonset hut where his men were passed out, turned on the lights, and shouted, "Are any of you guys drunk enough to come with me and bomb Rabaul tonight? Because that's what I'm doing and I'm taking off in fifteen minutes." Every man rose to the challenge. Some mumbled, "That sounds like fun," as they rolled out of bed.

VOLUNTEERS ONLY

Pappy Boyington had used Senge's three-point methodology to get his squadron "enrolled" in the mission. First, he had enrolled himself. He had clearly demonstrated that he was going to bomb Rabaul, whether or not anyone else came with him. Second, he was on the level with his men. Boyington did not try to soft-pedal the problem. He acknowledged that he was asking his men to do something crazy: to fly a combat mission while they were dead drunk.

> The Black Sheep—like most people—were far more inclined to do something if they did not feel they were being forced.

Finally, Boyington let his people choose. He made it clear that no one was obliged to go with him. The Black Sheep—like most people—were far more inclined to do something if they did not feel they were being forced.

COMMITMENT TO THE VISION

Sherry Ellingson also used the three-point enrollment method. She never pressured anyone to prospect online. But she let people know that she was doing it herself and gave them a realistic picture of how it worked for her. Then she backed off and allowed them to choose. Some tried it; most did not. For almost three years, Sherry's downline proceeded on autopilot, largely indifferent to the Internet.

In fact, Sherry's first big break in the business came without the help of online prospecting. About two and a half years into the business, Sherry noticed that one leg of her downline was growing faster than the others. In a four-month period, Sherry's commissions from that leg had grown from $1,000 to $8,000 per month. A gynecologist in Augusta, Georgia, working the business with his wife, had succeeded in recruiting many fellow doctors and was building his downline quickly.

Sherry was grateful for his success. Yet she did not want to work the business the same way that gynecologist did, using traditional prospecting methods. Sherry believed in her vision of an Internet-based business. She continued pursuing it, with the same resolve that Pappy Boyington had showed when he announced his plans to bomb Rabaul.

REINFORCEMENT

According to Senge, a vision spreads through an organization by means of a five-step reinforcement process:

1. **Early successes. The vision brings success to the first people who enroll in it.**
2. **Communication. People talk to other people, spreading the news about the vision and how it is working for others.**
3. **Clarification. The more people talk about the vision, the more clearly they understand it.**
4. **Enthusiasm. The more clearly they understand the vision, the more enthusiastic people grow.**
5. **Commitment. People begin committing to the vision. They adopt the vision as their own and demonstrate a willingness to put themselves on the line for it.**

Sherry's vision of an Internet-based Rexall business spread in precisely this way. Her success rate with online prospecting became the buzz of Sherry's downline. The more people talked about it, the more clearly they understood how it worked and its potential to help their business. Excitement grew. And as time went by, more and more people started trying it for themselves.

ALIGNMENT

When a team or company gets behind a vision, it is said to be in alignment. The difference between an aligned and unaligned team, says Senge, is like the difference between a laser beam and a light bulb. In a light bulb, the photons hurtle and collide in all different directions. As a result, the light is weak. In a laser beam, the photons all move in the same direction. All the energy of the light is focused. None is wasted. The beam is so strong, it can cut through solid metal in some cases.

"The fundamental characteristic of the relatively unaligned team is wasted energy," writes Senge. "Individuals may work extraordinarily hard, but their efforts do not efficiently translate to team effort. By contrast, when a team becomes more aligned, a commonality of direction emerges, and individuals' energies harmonize. There is less wasted energy."

THE MAGIC MOMENT

Before Sherry Ellingson's vision caught on, much energy was wasted in her downline. Everyone followed his or her own vision. There was little consensus on how to work the business. As a result, many people chose methods that were ineffective for them. "I had one particular distributor who struggled with this business for three years," says Sherry. "She put her heart and soul into it. I don't know anyone who worked harder than she did. But she had virtually no income." Then the woman started using Sherry's online prospecting techniques. Her income skyrocketed. Within weeks, her downline grew into one of Sherry's most productive legs.

Similar success stories emerged throughout Sherry's downline. "Other distributors started using the same online techniques that I did," says Sherry, "and they started getting the same success rate, the same sign-up ratios. This proved to me that it worked." Sherry's pump-priming days were over. All of a sudden, she saw growth in several different legs at once. "It used to be, I made a lot more outgoing calls than I received incoming calls," she says. "I always had to be on top of distributors, making sure people were doing what they were supposed to. But then it reversed. They were calling me, rather than me trying to track them down." Sherry was inundated by requests for help in training, support, and closing, from downline distributors who suddenly found themselves swamped with interested prospects. "Other distributors saw the success," she says. And they wanted to be part of it. Over a six-month period, Sherry's monthly commissions quintupled.

VISION FROM BELOW

"The first step in mastering the discipline of building shared visions," writes Senge, "is to give up traditional notions that visions are always announced from 'on high' or come from an organization's institutional planning processes." An enlightened leader must watch and listen, says Senge, to find out what his organization is trying to tell him. Sometimes, the best ideas emanate from below. In a healthy organization, "individuals not only feel free to express their dreams, but learn how to listen to each other's dreams. Out of this listening, new insights into what is possible gradually emerge."

That is what happened with Rexall. Without realizing it, Sherry became part of a much wider "visioning" process that ultimately changed the way Rexall does business. Like many MLM companies, Rexall had long discouraged its distributors from advertising on the Internet. There were good reasons for this policy. A network marketing company can be held legally liable for improper product or earnings claims made by its representatives online. Many companies take the safe way out by discouraging such activity altogether.

But Sherry and other sales leaders in Rexall were convinced they could find ways to promote the business online without causing problems for the company. They investigated and experimented with various online promotional methods for years, and lobbied Rexall executives to get behind Web-based prospecting. To its credit, upper management responded by formulating a new vision for the company.

REXALL.COM

In February 2000, Rexall became the first major MLM company to move its entire business online. "Rexall.com" enables distributors to conduct literally every aspect of their operations through the Internet.

In conventional MLM, distributors buy mailing lists, take out classified ads, or recruit friends, family, and associates. In Rexall.com, they use special e-marketing techniques to find leads through the Internet. Conventional network marketers present the business through videos or audiotapes, mailed or handed to prospects, or through live meetings. Rexall.com distributors refer prospects to a Web site for a multimedia presentation. Live training meetings—though still used—can now be replaced by online training and chat rooms. Gone are the days when Rexall forbade distributors to sell and prospect via Internet: Now every distributor gets a customized e-commerce Web site, provided by the company.

A VISION FULFILLED

For Sherry Ellingson, Rexall.com was the final step in fulfilling her vision. Before the program was launched, Sherry's online prospecting methods accomplished only half of the job. "I could make contacts online," she says, "but once I had them, I had to revert back to the old brick-and-mortar system of sending an audiotape and support material, building belief, and doing three-way phone calls with them. The magic of the new system is that everything's online."

Sherry feels no nostalgia for the days when she used to drive hours to give business presentations, only to find that no prospects had shown up. She doesn't miss stuffing packages with audiotapes and spending hours on the phone baby-sitting her downline. Sherry's vision of an easy-to-work home business has been realized in every detail. Now she shares that vision confidently with other women who are eager to duplicate her feat of becoming a financially independent, stay-at-home mom. Like Xenophon, Sherry held onto her dream through every hardship. And like the Ten Thousand, she has finally arrived at the sea.

The Seven Traits of an MLM Leader: Summary

Those who aspire to MLM leadership must cultivate seven essential character traits, as follows:

TRAIT NUMBER 1—DRIVE

Drive is another word for ambition. It is a hunger for success, a fire in your belly. Unlike the other six traits, drive is hard to acquire if you don't already have it. Some people gain ambition through financial hardship or humiliating setbacks. They are driven by the need to prove or redeem themselves. But many more are simply born with it. Drive gives you the power to overcome obstacles, slough off rejection, and endure disappointment.

TRAIT NUMBER 2—PERSISTENCE

Persistence is the habit of staying on course, despite all hardships. You achieve it by breaking down your task in small parts, so that you don't get overwhelmed. Deal with each task one at a time. As 1892 heavyweight boxing champion "Gentleman Jim" Corbett put it, "You become a champion by fighting one more round. When things are tough, you fight one more round."

TRAIT NUMBER 3—TEACHABILITY

Teachability is the habit of being humble. You must learn to follow before you can lead.

TRAIT NUMBER 4—THICK SKIN

Thick skin is the quality of being impervious to criticism. Every leader will be criticized. Since we are human, the criticism hurts. But a successful leader never changes his actions to please his critics. He understands that the critics do not share his goals. Listen to your critics, and you will serve their agenda, not your own.

TRAIT NUMBER 5—POSITIVE ATTITUDE

Positive thinking is the quality of being happy in your work. It comes from being so deeply absorbed in what you are doing that you literally do not have time to think discouraging thoughts. The best way to achieve this state is to treat your work as a game. There should be rules, goals, and some way of keeping score. The daily goals should be things that are under your control (such as the number of prospecting calls placed), rather than things you cannot control (such as how many sales you close). That way, you avoid frustration. Challenge yourself, each day, to "score" just a little higher than the day before. If the "game" is set up properly, you will become so deeply absorbed in it, you will not have time to dwell on worries, frustrations, or anxieties.

TRAIT NUMBER 6—COMPASSION

Compassion is not an emotion or a state of mind. It is action. A leader wins the loyalty of his troops by demonstrating, through actions, that he is looking out for their interests. He does this by providing his people with the tools they need to succeed; by praising people for their successes and blaming himself for their failures; and by pushing people only as hard as they are willing to push themselves. In return for these considerations, people will give you loyalty. They will work harder for a benevolent leader than they ever would for a despot.

TRAIT NUMBER 7—VISION

Vision is the ability to imagine a better future. It means setting goals and working steadily to achieve them. A leader never forgets his goals. He reminds himself of those goals everyday. At the same time, he also keeps a careful eye on reality. An effective leader always knows exactly how wide the gap is between his vision and his present reality. Ordinary people get discouraged when they contemplate that gap, but a leader is energized by it. It spurs him to keep striving for the better future he imagines.

PART THREE

THE WAVE 4 WAY

The Five Core Strategies of MLM Leadership

CHAPTER 14

The Skills of a Leader

In January 2000, Apple Computer founder, Steven Jobs, made a stunning announcement. He formally accepted the title of chief executive officer of Apple. The moment marked the climax of one of history's great comeback stories.

Jobs had been ousted from the top position at Apple fifteen years earlier. The company he built had declared him unfit to lead. It wasn't a question of ability. Jobs was obviously a genius. Starting from a garage in 1977, Jobs had built Apple into a billion-dollar corporation in six years, selling as many personal computers in 1983 as IBM.

But Jobs's methods left something to be desired. Wrapped up in his vision, Jobs tended to treat lesser mortals with brutal contempt. He screamed insults at executives in the middle of meetings. He drove people to exhaustion with impossible deadlines. When his own hand-picked management team finally ganged up on Jobs and ousted him, the company he created breathed a sigh of relief. Apple's stock shot through the roof.

But Jobs was not so easily dismissed. He was determined to make a comeback. Within a year of leaving Apple, Jobs started two new companies, NeXT and Pixar. Filled with confidence, he set out once more to conquer the world. But this time the task would prove much harder than before.

Jobs struggled for twelve years and invested tens of millions of dollars of his own money in his two companies before they finally paid off. He finally learned what it meant to prime the pump. In the process, he acquired many of the leadership skills that he had formerly lacked.

One executive recalled that Jobs still evinced many of his more obnoxious traits during the early years at Pixar. "After the first three words out of your mouth, he'd interrupt you and say, 'O.K., here's how I see things,'" she told the *New York Times* in 1997. "It isn't like that anymore. He listens a lot more, and he's more relaxed, more mature."

Jobs had learned from his mistakes. He was still the same man, inflamed by the same passions, driven by the same demons. But he had learned to temper the extremes of his personality with a leader's skills. And that changed everything for him.

> He had learned to temper the extremes of his personality with a leader's skills. And that changed everything for him.

During Jobs's twelve-year absence, his successors at Apple Computer had run the company into the ground. Its market share had plummeted to 3 percent by 1997. It had lost nearly $2 billion in the last two years. No one expected Apple Computer to survive. In desperation, the company that had rejected Steve Jobs begged him to come back.

The old Jobs would have jumped in with both feet. He would have crowed to the press about his vindication and strutted in triumph through the corridors of Apple Computer. He would have camped out in his office for twenty-hour stretches and forced everyone else to camp out with him. But Jobs had learned subtlety during his long exile. Now he played hard to get.

Jobs agreed only to step in as "interim CEO" for an indefinite period. He accepted only $1 per year in salary and worked only part time at Apple. The rest of his time he devoted to Pixar and his family. "I'm Apple's interim CEO, and it won't be forever," he told an interviewer in 1998. "I'm doing the best I can. If folks think there's a better solution, I'll be glad to step aside. And eventually, we'll find somebody else to take the reins." When *Business Week* asked Jobs whether his return would restore "a sense of magic" to Apple, Jobs retorted, "You're missing it. This is not a one-man show. . . . There's a lot of really talented people in this company. . . ."

> No matter how many mistakes you've made in the past, how many bridges you've burned, or how many people you've alienated, the opportunity is always there to begin anew.

For two and a half years, Jobs worked quietly at his task. And miraculously, Apple turned around. For the first time in years, the company began to innovate. It sold nearly two million units of the iMac in one year, making it the hottest personal computer on the market. Apple turned profitable again. Its stock hit record highs. Earnings in excess of a billion dollars are projected for 2000.

Steve Jobs had proved Eisenhower's adage that "The one quality that can develop by studious reflection and practice is the leadership of men." His twelve years in exile had made him a leader. Not only had he turned Apple around, but his other companies had become successful, too. NeXt Computer had been sold to Apple in 1996 for $400 million. Pixar's partnership with Disney was the talk of Hollywood, yielding blockbusters such as *A Bug's Life* and *Toy Story I* and *II*. The brash young boy with the abrasive management style had become a skilled executive.

You can work a similar alchemy in your own life. No matter how many mistakes you've made in the past, how many bridges you've burned, or how many people you've alienated, the opportunity is always there to begin anew. It is simply a matter of applying yourself to "studious reflection" and "practice."

The previous section focused on the character of a leader. Now we will explore the specific strategies that leaders use to harness and direct the efforts of other people. I have identified three strategies that seem to be used by virtually all successful network marketers. It may not be realistic to expect such a fairy-tale turnaround as Steven Jobs enjoyed. But the Five Core Strategies of MLM Leadership will empower you to take charge of your downline. Whether or not you have been effective or ineffective in handling people in the past, the application of these techniques will enable you to do a better job in the future.

CHAPTER 15

Strategy Number 1— Build a Team

As previously noted, the fact that America survived the Civil War intact can be attributed largely to Abraham Lincoln's personal determination and leadership skills. But that does not mean Lincoln did it single-handedly. He had plenty of help. Indeed, team-building was one of Lincoln's most important skills.

When the war began, Lincoln did not have the right people in place. It showed on the battlefield. Lincoln's plan was to attack the Southern armies aggressively and repeatedly until they were annihilated. But none of his generals shared this vision. As described by management expert Donald T. Phillips in his book, *Lincoln on Leadership,* their strategies were consistently defensive in nature.

General George B. McClellan refused to attack the Confederates for months at a time. Without constant prodding from Lincoln, he might never have engaged the enemy at all. General George Meade was not much better. He won a great victory for the Union at Gettysburg. But after the battle, Lincoln was enraged to discover that Meade, instead of pursuing Lee's army and destroying it, had merely ordered his men to "Drive from our soil every vestige of the presence of the invader."

"Drive the invader from our soil?" cried Lincoln. "My God! Is that all? . . . Will our generals never get that idea out of their heads? The whole country is our soil." Because Meade did not share Lincoln's determination to annihilate the Southern armies, he allowed Robert E. Lee to escape Gettysburg with his army intact.

FIND YOUR GRANT

Lincoln went through many different commanders before settling on Ulysses S. Grant. It was a controversial appointment. Grant was severely criticized for his many alleged faults, such as drunkenness and disregard for human life (his casualties were always high). But Lincoln responded: "I can't spare this man. He fights!"

Because he was a fighter, Grant attracted other fighters to his team, such as William Tecumseh Sherman. Only a year after Grant was given command of the Union Army, the war was over. It might have ended a lot sooner, had Grant been appointed at the very beginning of the conflict.

Building a winning team may have been the single most important act of Lincoln's career. He succeeded because he refused to give up until he had found the right people. "Keep searching until you find your 'Grant,'" advises Phillips in *Lincoln on Leadership*.

> Building a winning team may have been the single most important act of Lincoln's career. He succeeded because he refused to give up until he had found the right people.

CATCH A BIG FISH

Team-building is just as crucial in network marketing as it was on the Civil War battlefield. The goal is to "catch a big fish"—another way of saying, "Find your Grant." It means recruiting someone into your downline who has such impressive resources, contacts, energy, sales talent—or all the above—that he quickly builds a profitable organization beneath you.

Just as Ulysses S. Grant attracted aggressive commanders to his team, such as Sherman, so your "big fish" will tend to attract other big fish, who will attract others in turn. Assembling a core group of leaders is a crucial first step toward building a self-sufficient downline, one that will grow and sustain itself for years to come, even without your direct involvement.

SELF-HELP CRUSADER

As this book goes to press, a particularly revealing example of the "big fish" principle has been getting attention in the national media. The big fish is Tony Brown, a bestselling African-American author, journalist, and host of *Tony Brown's Journal,* the longest-running show on PBS. Brown preaches a message of self-reliance, urging black Americans to lift themselves up through entrepreneurship. He sees network marketing as one way of putting his self-help gospel into action.

A distributor for Pre-Paid Legal Services, Inc., Brown says, "I've got 20,000 people that I've put in business. I haven't found another way [besides Pre-Paid Legal] to put this many black people into business."

Brown was recruited by Jonathan Blount, a prominent African-American businessman and Pre-Paid Legal distributor. In persuading Brown to join his downline, Blount had caught a very big fish indeed. Tony Brown's celebrity and media access made him a powerful recruiter. As with Ulysses S. Grant, many of the fish Brown reeled in turned out to be just as big, in their own way, as Brown himself.

THE CRUSADE

A large part of the appeal that Pre-Paid Legal exerts toward big fish like Tony Brown is the fact that it sells more than a product. It sells a crusade. "In America today, you're going to get as much justice as you can pay for," explains founder, chairman, and CEO Harland C. Stonecipher. "What we're doing is changing the system. We're getting it down to where the average middle-income working American can afford justice."

The Ada, Oklahoma, company is a kind of HMO for legal services. It maintains a network of some 30,000 law firms across the country. For a small monthly fee, clients get access to a range of legal services, including contract reviews, will preparation, and phone consultations, as well as partial coverage for trials, car accidents, and tax audits. The fee varies from state to state, but a basic package (without trial defense or IRS coverage) goes for $13.95 a month in New York.

THE DISTRIBUTION CHALLENGE

The concept was born in 1969, when Stonecipher got in a head-on collision. His car and hospital bills were covered by insurance but not his legal expenses. That got Stonecipher thinking. An insurance salesman by trade, he conceived the idea of a legal HMO and launched the new company in 1972. The product was good, but the market was slow to respond. After ten years of sluggish growth, Stonecipher decided to try MLM. Sales doubled from $4 to $8 million in one year. The second year, they doubled again.

Pre-Paid Legal is now one of the hottest companies on the stock market. For the five-year period beginning in 1993, it was the number one offering on the American Stock Exchange, in terms of profit growth (the company has since been listed on the New York Stock Exchange). In 1999, *Money* magazine ranked it the thirteenth best-performing stock of the 1990s (Microsoft was only number 17). Sales for 1999 were an estimated $150 million. With a 48-percent rise in the recruitment rate last year, the company now has over 200,000 independent distributors.

REINVENTING THE HAMBURGER

Stonecipher is fond of comparing his success to that of Ray Kroc, the founder of McDonald's. And the two men do share much in common. Both succeeded not so much because they sold a unique product, but because they found a unique way to distribute it.

"Ray Kroc didn't invent the hamburger," says Stonecipher. "He didn't invent the hamburger restaurant. There were plenty of them out there. But he changed the method of delivery. And that's what made McDonald's successful." Stonecipher similarly did not invent lawyers or legal insurance. But, like Kroc, Stonecipher found an innovative way to deliver his service. Where Kroc used franchising, Stonecipher employs network marketing.

BEYOND MCDONALD'S

Network marketing resembles franchising, in that it relies on a network of independent contractors. Such decentralized structures enable a company to grow at lightning speed. Take McDonald's. Back in 1955, it was an unknown burger stand in California. America's leading hamburger chain was White Castle, with 27 stores. Thirty years later, McDonald's boasted 8,278 outlets to White Castle's 167.

McDonald's grew faster because it used franchising. Each time White Castle added a store, it had to invest its own money. But McDonald's franchisees were independent entrepreneurs. They paid the start-up costs themselves. Network marketers also pay their own way. They proliferate even faster than franchisees, because their start-up costs are less. A franchisee might spend millions to put up a store in a prime retail location. The average Pre-Paid Legal representative can get started for about $249.

Stonecipher views MLM as a natural extension of franchising. And he views himself as an extension of Ray Kroc. Whenever he needs guidance, Stonecipher pulls out his smudged and dog-eared copy of Kroc's autobiography, *Grinding It Out*. Every page is filled with underlinings and margin notes. A previous copy of the book fell apart from constant use.

"I am a disciple of Ray Kroc," declares Stonecipher. "Kroc's unique ability was to take independent contractors and get them to follow a set of rules and guidelines and work together." Stonecipher believes he has done something similar with Pre-Paid Legal.

QUALITY CONTROL

Of course, Stonecipher did not invent MLM, any more than Ray Kroc invented franchising. Both men simply ironed out the bugs in an existing system. But that was enough. Even today, many companies let their franchisees run wild. Ray Kroc kept his on a short leash. Company inspectors made sure that every franchise owner followed the rules. To this day, customers can expect the same level of cleanliness, courtesy, quality, and fast service at any McDonald's outlet, from Moscow to Kuala Lumpur.

Stonecipher, too, runs a tight ship. He appoints regional vice presidents in every state to enforce compliance with company standards. Anyone caught violating company rules or flouting state and federal regulations is quickly spotted and reprimanded. If the violation is serious or persistent, the sales associate may be terminated.

Stonecipher's quality control program extends even to the law firms in his network. Lawyers and support personnel from participating firms must take customer service courses from Pre-Paid Legal. Customers are surveyed every forty-five days, to make sure the firm is meeting their needs. Even phone traffic is monitored from Pre-Paid Legal headquarters, through a proprietary phone system that every firm is required to install.

"We monitor them on a daily basis," says Stonecipher. "On any given day, I can tell you how many calls they've taken at a particular law firm, and how many times the phone rang before they picked it up. If it rings more than three times, that's too many. At the end of the day, I can see how many people called that day and have not yet talked to a lawyer. If those people haven't all been able to talk to a lawyer, then we're going to be checking on that and see why not."

EXERCISING INITIATIVE

Long before he was given command of the Union Army, Ulysses S. Grant distinguished himself on the battlefield. In 1862, he was given the nickname "Unconditional Surrender" Grant, for his forceful actions in Tennessee. Grant's relentless campaign against Vicksburg cut the Confederacy in two. Lincoln took note of these victories. He kept a careful eye on Grant for more than two years. Finally, in 1864, Lincoln placed Grant in command of all Union forces.

It was a wise decision. Grant immediately presented Lincoln with a plan to launch a coordinated attack of all Union armies against the Confederacy. "Grant is the first general I have had," Lincoln commented. "You know how it has been with all the rest. They wanted me to be the general. I am glad to find a man who can go ahead without me."

You will recognize your "Grant" by the fact that he takes the initiative and goes ahead without you. With little or no direction from above, he will formulate plans and execute them with vigor. All you need to do is turn him loose to do what he does best.

NICHE MARKETS

Much like Grant, Tony Brown took the initiative in his campaign to bring Pre-Paid Legal Services to New York. Traditionally, network marketers have viewed New York City as one of the hardest markets to penetrate. The conventional wisdom is that busy New Yorkers don't have time to attend opportunity meetings, and their skeptical nature makes them resistant to sales pitches. But Tony Brown has forced the industry to rethink its view of the Big Apple. He has made New York one of the fastest-growing markets for Pre-Paid Legal.

Key to Brown's success has been putting together the right team. One of the first fish he reeled in was Ron Diaz, a native of Trinidad who had struck it rich in America, through MLM. "Tony Brown called me Superbowl Sunday 1997," remembers Diaz. "I said, 'Tony, my plate is full. I can't look at another business.' And Tony Brown, with all his wisdom, paused for a moment and said, 'Your plate is full with the wrong kind of food. Why don't you come down here and look at some real food?'"

Diaz was persuaded to join. He, in turn, combed his Rolodex and started calling other MLM sales leaders. The combination of Brown's celebrity and Diaz's business reputation proved an irresistible lure. Diaz quickly assembled a winning sales team. More than 5,000 people joined Brown's downline in the first six months. "New York began to really take off," Stonecipher recalls.

> You will recognize your "Grant" by the fact that he takes the initiative and goes ahead without you.

Diaz subsequently organized a sales rally at New York's Waldorf-Astoria hotel. There was standing-room only in the Grand Ballroom, with 2,600 people in attendance. Brown and Stonecipher met there for the first time. The two men hit it off immediately. "I liked the guy," says Stonecipher. "I liked his ideas. He was saying, 'We don't need government hand-outs. We can do it on our own, if we're given the opportunity.'"

THE LEGAL SHIELD

Shortly after joining Pre-Paid Legal, Brown heard an intriguing story from one of his sales leaders. Four black teenagers had been arrested in New York. While searching them, police found a Pre-Paid Legal membership card on one of the youths. "They pulled him aside and told him to go home," says Brown. The other three were thrown in jail, according to the sales leader.

That and other incidents got Brown thinking. He had already started educating Stonecipher about racial profiling: the practice of detaining, questioning, and even arresting suspects based on little more than race. Now Brown sensed a solution. He and Stonecipher put their heads together in a series of brainstorming sessions. They came up with the idea of a membership card with some extra kick in it: the Legal Shield.

For an additional dollar per month (and for no extra cost in New York), policy holders would get a card imprinted with a toll-free number to a local law firm. The card warns that "This person is a member of the Legal Shield program and has 24-hour access to legal representation." Clients being detained by police are instructed to show the card to the arresting officer. In theory, it discourages police officers from arresting or searching you without due cause.

"The Legal Shield levels the playing field," says Stonecipher. "We don't need more laws. There are plenty of laws out there. What we need is to give people access to the law. And we have a method that works, through the free enterprise system."

The Legal Shield creates no bureaucracies, spawns no regulations, and squanders no tax dollars. It simply puts cops on notice that they must watch their p's and q's. More than 100,000 cards have been sold since the program was rolled out in September. A large proportion have gone to New York City minorities.

GRASSROOTS SELLING

MLM's unique approach to team-building has played a considerable role in the success of the Legal Shield program. On its own, Pre-Paid Legal might never have recognized disgruntled urban minorities as a potential customer base, any more than Abraham Lincoln could have won the Civil War without Grant.

Indeed, protecting blacks and Hispanics from "racial profiling" is about as far from Pre-Paid's core business as you can get. Middle-class, white-collar professionals have been its meat and potatoes since the company began. But network marketing encourages individual initiative from the ranks. Enterprising distributors, such as Tony Brown, have the ability to influence company policy through their words and actions. They also have the best access to the market, through their circle of personal acquaintances.

LASER-LIKE FOCUS

Brown's downline is 80 percent African-American. This sort of laser-like focus is invaluable for selling specialized products, such as the Legal Shield. But Brown achieved it without even trying. "That's the way network marketing works," Brown explains. "You go to people you know and say, 'Hey, I've got a great idea. You want to get in on it?' And then your friend goes to his buddies and says the same thing. If people are recruiting their friends and relatives, you're always going to get Koreans bringing in Koreans, Italians bringing in Italians, and so forth."

On a smaller scale, Brown's feat is duplicated each day by hundreds of thousands of independent Pre-Paid Legal distributors, each one reaching friends, family, neighbors, and co-workers. Whether he is white, black, urban, suburban, middle class, working class, famous, or obscure, each distributor can reach the market closest to him with a directness impossible through mass-media advertising.

Brown put his downline to work. Brown dispatched thousands of independent distributors into black neighborhoods. They told their friends and families about Legal Shield and recruited others to do the same.

Brown also hawked the service through his Web site and radio show. The *New York Daily News* obligingly ran his phone number in an article about the Legal Shield program. "Response has been excellent," Brown told the *Daily News* in March. "You don't have to tell black people that they need it. It's like, 'Where can I sign?'"

Propelled largely by word-of-mouth, the program is spreading rapidly around the country. "I don't think we've seen anything yet," says Stonecipher. "The Legal Shield is not just for minorities. What we're doing is changing the way the legal system works. No one can call a lawyer at three o'clock in the morning, not even the wealthy. But the Legal Shield lets you do that."

TEAMWORK

Frustrated with General George G. McClellan's failure to act, Lincoln remarked to his friend, Orville Browning, in 1862, "I am thinking of taking the field myself." He actually did, at one point, in May of that year, as recounted in Phillips' *Lincoln on Leadership*.[1] Lincoln traveled to Fort Monroe and took personal command of Union forces there. He ordered an artillery bombardment of the Confederate batteries at Sewall's Point. Then Lincoln personally scouted for a good spot for an amphibious landing. When he found one, he ordered an attack on Norfolk, Virginia. It succeeded and the town was taken.

Perhaps Lincoln was thinking of this incident later when, after Meade allowed Lee to escape from Gettysburg, Lincoln complained bitterly to his son Robert that had he been there personally, "I could have whipped them myself." The temptation is always great for a leader, to step in and do things himself. But effective leaders understand that you can accomplish far more with a team than you can alone. In your MLM business, you will often feel, like Lincoln, that you are surrounded by people who don't share your passion and drive. The solution is not to step in and do the business for them. It is to keep searching until you find your "Grant."

1. All of the anecdotes about Lincoln in *The Wave 4 Way* are taken from Phillips' excellent book.

16

Strategy Number 2— Train Your People

At some point in any network marketing business, you will wake up one morning and say to yourself, "Who am I going to talk to today?" You have already pitched the business to your friends and family. People at work are starting to walk the other way when they see you coming. As far as you can tell, you have exhausted every potential prospect within your personal sphere of influence.

You call your sponsor to ask what to do. He just impatiently tells you to get out there and start meeting people. This is the point where many otherwise promising and well-motivated networkers leave the business. They leave not because they are discouraged or lazy, but simply because they do not know what to do next, and no one will tell them.

Knowing how to help people through this crisis is a key skill for MLM leaders. It can mean all the difference between having a successful downline, where people stay with you for years, or having a revolving-door downline where your best people give up and leave almost as fast as they get started.

A REVOLVING DOOR

Jerry Campisi experienced that revolving-door phenomenon when he first got into networking. Today, he and his wife,

Debbie, are top sales leaders with Big Planet, a company selling Internet access and other high-tech products and services. But getting there was not easy.

After twenty years as a business and financial consultant, Jerry thought he knew the business world pretty well. But his background ill-prepared him for the special demands of MLM leadership.

"I didn't understand the business," he admits. "Everyone I listened to and all the books on networking that I read all said the same thing: Talk to people you know and people you know of." Jerry dutifully passed these instructions down to his recruits. But after a few months, he realized there was a problem.

> **K**nowing how to help people through this [revolving-door] crisis is a key skill for MLM leaders.

"I was losing people," he says. "They were running into a stone wall and quitting. People in my group were telling me that they had already gone through everyone they knew." Particularly discouraging for Jerry was the fact that some of his best, most persistent people were leaving. Typically in MLM, the vast majority of networkers drop out within a few days or weeks, without really trying. But Jerry found that over 20 percent of his recruits were leaving after sticking with the business for four to six months. These were not quitters. They were good people who just didn't know what to do next.

TRAINING PROGRAM

Jerry's people needed alternatives. They needed creative and innovative methods of finding fresh prospects. But the existing literature on MLM offered few such alternatives. Most of it consisted of the same tired exhortations about talking to everyone you know. It did not tell you how to move beyond who you knew, into the wide world of the cold market. So Jerry set out to devise his own training program.

He used trial and error. Making himself the guinea pig, Jerry experimented with different methods of prospecting. Any method that seemed to bear fruit, he passed on to his downline and urged his people to try it. Over a two-year period, Jerry amassed an impressive list of prospecting methods. When people came to Jerry complaining that they'd gone through their circle of influence and run out of prospects, he had an answer for them. He could offer a smorgasbord of methods for reaching new prospects, outside their warm market. People could pick and choose the methods that worked best for them.

Providing Alternatives

The mere fact that alternatives were available encouraged many people who would otherwise have left to stick with the business. More important, once those people started applying the new methods, they achieved results. Previously sluggish downlines began picking up speed and growing. After more than three years in the business, Jerry realized that he was starting to gain momentum. His Magic Moment had arrived.

"My business exploded," says Jerry. "Sales jumped 50 percent. I immediately started retaining about 15 to 20 percent more people than before." Today, as a distributor for Big Planet—a company based in Provo, Utah, that sells Internet service and high-tech products—Jerry presides over a multimillion-dollar sales organization.

Different Strokes for Different Folks

Traditional network marketing forces people into a cookie-cutter mold. Everyone must work the business in the same way. That means working your warm market and holding opportunity meetings in hotel conference rooms, where you have to get up and speak before crowds. For many people, such methods are off-putting. But that does not necessarily mean they cannot work the business.

Jerry once recruited a man who had made money in construction and had taken two years off to sail around the world with his wife in his sixty-foot yacht. He was living on his yacht in Fort Lauderdale, Florida, when Jerry met him. Because the man was from out of state, he did not know anyone locally. Moreover, he was shy. "He was an introvert," Jerry recalls. "He could never approach people cold. He could never stand up and do a meeting."

TRIGGERING THE MIND

In earlier years, Jerry might have lost this man. But now Jerry was offering regular training seminars to his downline, in which he presented them with alternatives. At one such seminar, Jerry told his trainees to think about running classified ads in magazines targeting people with special interests or renting subscriber lists from those publications to get leads. Since Big Planet was selling Internet service, Jerry suggested computer magazines as a good place to start.

The shy man with the yacht was listening. A light bulb went on in his head. After the seminar, he came up to Jerry and said, "You triggered my mind with something I can do. I know sailing. I know the mindset of a sailor. I know a lot of people with sailboats are looking to earn extra income. I could run a classified ad in a sailboat magazine and talk to those people about sailing and be able to bond with them, then offer the opportunity. I feel confident in that circle of people." The method worked for him. "He built a giant business with that one idea," says Jerry. Simply by offering multiple alternatives, Jerry had stimulated the man to start thinking for himself.

TURNING LEMONS INTO LEMONADE

You don't have to offer ready-made answers to everyone. Most people are smart enough to pick up the ball, once you pass it to them. Get people thinking about alternative prospecting methods and most will start coming up with their own ideas. They will apply their own ingenuity to their personal situations, often surprising you by the creative ways they discover to exploit even the most difficult circumstances.

Jerry recalls a truck driver in his downline who spent most of his time driving back and forth, from coast to coast. How would a person in this situation ever manage to sell an Internet-based business? But as Jerry patiently laid alternatives before the man, the truck driver's mind started working.

> Get people thinking about alternative prospecting methods and most will start coming up with their own ideas.

Two weeks after the man joined, Jerry started getting calls from leads the truck driver had recruited. Jerry was curious as to how he was doing it. He called the man up and asked him. "It's simple," said the truck driver. "I own my own rig, and I'm in the truck all day long. Every day, I'm driving by people who are business people. So I put an advertisement right on the side of the truck and on my mudflaps that says, 'I'm making money on the Internet right now. If you're not, call me. My cell is on.'" If an interested prospect calls on his cell phone, the man can pull over at any truck stop, most of which now provide Internet plug-ins, enabling him to do his multimedia sales presentation.

"I can't guarantee success for anyone," says Jerry. "What works for one person may not work for another. But I can offer people different ways of working the business, not just one way." That has made all the difference for Jerry's organization. And it could make the difference for yours.

MEMORY JOGGERS

One of the easiest and simplest ways you can help your recruits is to provide memory joggers when they are drawing up their warm lists. Every network marketer begins his business by making a list of friends, family, and associates who might be good prospects. But few people realize just how far their Circle of Influence extends. A few helpful hints can jog loose long-buried memories and help networkers double or triple the size of their lists.

Memory Jogger Number 1—Past Co-Workers

Tell your prospects to think back on every company that they have worked for in recent years and draw up a list of all their co-workers at those establishments. Managers and people in administrative positions—even secretaries—are particularly likely to have a comprehensive list in their heads of everyone who worked there. As the list grows, they find themselves remembering people whom they may not have thought of for years. These are all potential prospects.

Memory Jogger Number 2—Past Neighbors

Ask your prospects to think back on every place they have lived in recent years, and to envision in their minds their old neighborhoods and neighbors.

Memory Jogger Number 3—Scan the Atlas

If you have moved around a lot, it sometimes helps to flip through an atlas of the United States. As your eye wanders around the page, you will suddenly remember some brief incident in your life when you worked in a little town in Utah, say, or that summer you spent in the Florida Keys. Triggering these memories will help you remember people associated with these times in your life, with whom you may have fallen out of touch in the meantime.

Memory Jogger Number 4—
High School and College Yearbooks

People whom you went to school with are good prospects. More often than not, they will be intrigued to hear from some long-lost classmate. Flipping through old copies of your high school and college yearbooks is a great way to refresh your memory of these old acquaintances. You can also get in touch with whomever is in charge of organizing reunions for your class. That person will have a comprehensive list with updated phone numbers and addresses. If you have an old classmate you'd like to call but don't have contact information, you can sometimes find that person through the Internet, by searching sites such as whowhere.lycos.com.

COLD MARKET

No matter how diligently you jog your memory, eventually you will run out of acquaintances. Your warm market will be exhausted. If you want more leads, you will have to get them from the cold market. That means finding and prospecting perfect strangers. How do you do it? Jerry Campisi has found the following methods effective in amassing leads.

Classified Ads

Unfortunately, the most popular methods of working the cold market are also the most costly. "Classified ads are expensive," says Jerry Campisi. "It's one of the most expensive ways to market." Yet it brings results. A well-worded ad can enable you to sit at home and take calls from interested prospects. The prospects are already pre-qualified, because no one would respond to an ad unless he or she was seriously interested in your opportunity.

Before running classified ads, check with your company. Many MLM firms stipulate that classified ads must be generic, which is to say that they must not mention the name of the company. Other companies do not allow such ads at all. Jerry emphasizes that classified ads can be used to sell both the product and the opportunity. Product-oriented ads can be placed in special sections of the paper or in specialized publications, appropriate to the product, such as those related to health or beauty.

Direct Mail

Direct mail shares many of the advantages of classified advertising, in that it enables you to prospect from home and to wait for callbacks from interested prospects. As with classified advertising, the prospects who call will be pre-qualified. Unless they had a strong interest in your offer, they would not have responded to your mailing.

But, like classified advertising, direct mail is costly. You will have to purchase mailing lists from list brokers. You will have to stuff envelopes with flyers, videos, and audiotapes, all of which have to be paid for, and then pay for postage as well. Even after spending all that money, you may not get good results. Direct mail is an art form. It takes skill to write an effective marketing letter and to select a good mailing list. "If you're using direct mail, it is important not to mass-mail to unqualified leads," says Jerry. "Don't just mail blindly to anyone. Your list should be targeted."

He suggests that anyone trying direct mail should spend some time in the library first, reading how-to books on the subject and combing through the Standard Rate and Data directory, to see what lists are available.

Buttons

One method of advertising that costs almost nothing is to wear a button. "A lot of people laugh at buttons," says Jerry, "but they can get a response." In his Big Planet business, Jerry recommends buttons that say something like,

"I'm making money from the Internet right now. If you're not, ask me how."

"If you can get a person to respond to a button, then 50 percent of the sale is done right there," says Jerry. "You know they will be qualified."

T-Shirts

Like buttons, T-shirts bearing your sales message can be produced at very low cost. Jerry recommends attending events where you are likely to meet prospects, such as county fairs and trade shows, and circulating around while wearing your T-shirt. "Go where you feel your market is," says Jerry, "and your T-shirt does the selling for you."

Bumper Stickers

Check with your company before using bumper stickers. Many companies prefer that this very public form of advertising be done generically, without using the company name. Even so, it can draw many prospects. "Your car goes with you everywhere you go," says Jerry. "You can be getting advertising even when your car is parked at work all day." He also recommends placing advertising messages on windshield sun blockers.

COLD-CALLING

Cold-calling—another name for calling on perfect strangers—intimidates many salespeople. But it can be effective, especially if you choose your prospects with care. Some of Jerry Campisi's most successful methods involve targeting select groups of people for a cold-calling campaign.

Local Marriages in Newspaper

Young couples just starting out make excellent prospects. They have energy, ambition, high hopes, and usually financial need. Marriages are reported regularly in local newspapers.

Jerry recommends going to the library and getting the names of newlywed couples from six-month-old newspapers on microfiche.

"I go back six months because I want to get them after they're a little settled," Jerry explains. He calls up and says, "Look, I know you just got married six months ago, congratulations. You're probably both working right now, but would you be interested in taking a look at an Internet home business that you could operate yourself? If you decide to have children at some point, one of your incomes will stop, and this is a way that you could still have an income stream." Jerry reports high success rates in cold-calling newly married couples.

Bankruptcies

Most networkers would never suspect that people whose businesses have gone bankrupt make great prospects. "The fact that they went bankrupt does not mean they were bad businesspeople," says Jerry. "They might have gone bankrupt because of a partner problem, a divorce. It could be the economy. They are great, great potential distributors, because they want to replace their old lifestyle."

Often, you find such people working at temporary jobs just to survive. They are usually looking for a way out. As a network marketer, you have an ideal offer for such people: a business opportunity with a high upside and a low downside—high potential return, low investment.

In many communities, business bankruptcies are listed in the library on microfiche. Jerry recommends starting with bankruptcies from six months back, so that the person has had time to get over the initial shock and start thinking about his next move. Real estate bankruptcies are usually listed in the town hall. "If you owned property and you defaulted on that property, it's listed somewhere," says Jerry.

Once you have your leads, just get on the phone and start cold-calling. Jerry tells his bankrupt prospects, "I know you've been an open-minded business person. I have a business that has a high return, low investment. I don't know whether the time is right, but would you be interested in taking a look at it?" A surprisingly high number respond positively, says Jerry.

People Who Deal with Business People

Jerry recommends targeting salesmen who sell to businesspeople. Once you've recruited such a person, all his leads become your leads. In this group, Jerry includes insurance agents, stockbrokers, real estate agents, even car salesmen. "I like to look for the people who are the top players in each of these industries, because I know the top 20 percent are not happy," says Jerry. "They usually want more, or they don't want to work weekends or whatever."

In many cases, you can simply look these people up in the Yellow Pages and start calling. But walk-ins are also effective. With car salesmen, for instance, Jerry likes to show up personally at the showroom, especially where pricier cars are being sold. Perceiving Jerry as a potential customer, the salesman will approach him. One of the first things the salesman is likely to ask is, "What sort of business are you in?"

"He's trying to bond with you and find out if you're qualified to buy the car," Jerry explains. So you tell him about your business, say you're looking for sales representatives in the area, and ask him if he's interested in diversifying his income. If he decides to join your business, you're in luck. Most car salesmen keep lists of leads, many of whom are substantial businesspeople.

> In network marketing, it always helps to have access to large numbers of people.

Property Managers

In network marketing, it always helps to have access to large numbers of people. Property managers have access to more than most, because they know everyone who lives or works in the buildings they manage. Jerry recommends simply calling up building complexes and asking for the managers. Lists of property managers can also be found in directories in the library.

NETWORKING OR "THE SOCIAL APPROACH"

This approach involves putting yourself in social situations, bonding with people, and presenting them with your opportunity. The types of situations may vary from a business or motivational seminar to a church, school, or community event.

Some examples follow.

Walking and Talking

This involves simply walking around in high-traffic areas where professional people are likely to be—for instance, public squares or malls where businesspeople come during their lunch hours, business and trade shows, and so on—and striking up conversations with people. You can use an indirect approach, in which you bond with the person by striking up a conversation on some other subject, or the direct approach, where you simply tell the person up front that you would like to interest him or her in a business opportunity.

The goal is not to engage the person in a prolonged conversation (which many prospects might find annoying) but simply to exchange business cards and hopefully leave the prospect with a sales aid, such as a video, audiotape, or CD-ROM business card (see "Tools or Sales Aids," further on).

"Don't do the selling there," cautions Jerry. "The object is to exchange business cards. And you should use a generic business card, meaning that it doesn't say much, so that you get them to call. If you tell people everything, then they don't need to talk to you again, because they can make a decision based on what you give them. It's hard to explain your product or service in a short period of time."

Obviously, this sort of approach requires a certain gregariousness and works better in some areas than in others. If you buttonhole someone on the street in the middle of midtown Manhattan, for instance, your prospect might react by grabbing hold of his wallet and looking around for a cop. But Jerry says the method is surprisingly effective in more low-pressure environments, where people don't mind being approached.

"I personally like to go to the nothing-down real estate deals, the motivation seminars," says Jerry. "The reason why people are going to these events is they want to improve their situation." After-work happy hours in upscale bars are also a good hunting ground, says Jerry.

Lifestyle Marketer

In social networking, the goal is to get your prospect to ask what you do. One good way to accomplish this is to ask the prospect what *he* does for a living. After he tells you, he will probably ask the same question of you in return.

If Jerry can get a prospect to ask this question, he often responds by saying, "I'm a lifestyle marketer." Then he falls silent. The prospect will then ask what that means. That is your opening to begin explaining your network marketing business. If you sense interest, you can get right down to business. Ask the prospect if he can use some extra money. Ask if he has a cassette player in his car to listen to an audiotape on his way home. And, by all means, exchange business cards.

Join Clubs and Associations

A great way to meet people is to join clubs, such as Kiwanis, women's clubs, or the local chamber of commerce. Such clubs encourage new members to introduce themselves at the meetings. This gives you a great selling opportunity. "I wouldn't do hard-core selling in that situation," says Jerry.

"Just tell them that you're a new member and explain what you have, more in an informational or explanatory way than a selling way." Tell them just enough to arouse curiosity. Through such clubs it is possible to reach important business and community leaders, with a wide circle of influence.

Speak at Breakfast Clubs

Many clubs and organizations sponsor breakfast meetings devoted to a theme. Volunteer as a guest speaker at these events and talk about your product or service. Be informative. No hard selling. If you're selling Internet service, talk about the Internet. If you're selling nutritional products, talk about health issues. Tell them just enough to spark curiosity about your product or opportunity. Those with an interest will approach you after your talk.

PROACTIVE EVENTS

Of course, you don't have to wait for someone else to throw an event. You can be proactive and create your own. Jerry and his team have had success with the following concepts:

Entrepreneurial or Business Luncheons

Throw a business lunch, where you are the guest speaker. Get people to come by offering them a free lunch. Restaurants will be glad to cut you a deal for a back room or private room since you are bringing in so many people. If the event is well-run, the money you make from recruiting will more than compensate you for the cost of the lunch. You can also split the cost of the lunch with any of your downline leaders who attend, since they, too, will be using it as a hunting ground.

Professional people like to attend luncheons where they know they will be meeting and networking with their peers. You might try devoting certain luncheons to particular professions, such as real estate agents or CPAs.

Seminars

The key to marketing through seminars is to provide real value to your customers. No one wants to go out of his way to attend a seminar if the event is just a camouflaged sales pitch. Your goal must be to ensure that people go away satisfied, whether or not they end up buying your product or service or joining your downline.

As an example, Jerry points to one leader in his downline who is capitalizing on his Internet experience. This fellow offers free seminars on how to get a Web site up and running. He invites local businesspeople and advertises his seminars in the newspaper. Whether or not attendees end up subscribing to his Internet service or joining his organization, everyone who attends his seminar gets what he came for, which is to learn how to put up a Web page.

> As with support groups, the key to marketing through seminars is to provide real value to your customers.

"He teaches them what he said he would teach them," says Jerry. "But now he has a customer base of businesspeople who are going on the Internet. Now he'll cross-market to them afterward through a letter. If they're interested in making money on the Internet, he's already developed a relationship with them."

TOOLS OR SALES AIDS

Critical to your success in networking—whether at social or proactive events—is having the right tools or sales aids at your disposal. When you find an interested prospect, you should have some sort of promotional material on hand to give him or her. A few examples follow:

Professional Business Card

A business card is the most basic prospecting tool. Yet many networkers neglect it. They produce cheap, unoriginal cards that fail to make an impression, or worse, make a bad impression. You should treat your business card as an important advertisement for your product and opportunity.

> You should treat your business card as an important advertisement for your product and opportunity.

"I personally believe that you should not put anything on your card that doesn't look professional to any potential distributor or customer," says Jerry. "If you're going to have a business card, make it professional. And don't just put your name on it. Tell them something that will trigger them to respond."

As examples, Jerry suggests: "Hottest business opportunity of the 2000s," "Call our 24-hour hotline," "Live healthy and prosper," "Improve your health and make money at the same time," "Capitalize on tomorrow's technology today," and so on.

Picture Business Card

For a little extra money, you can spruce up your card with a picture. "There is more response to a picture business card than to a regular one," says Jerry. A picture of you helps build a connection with your prospect. You can also put a "lifestyle" picture on your card: a shot of your home, perhaps, or some other scene that evokes the prosperous lifestyle that successful networkers can enjoy.

Talking Business Card

If you want to get really fancy, you can have business cards made that read off a fifteen- to twenty-second recorded message at the press of a button. A small chip on the back provides the sound. It might say something as simple as, "Hi, this is Jerry Campisi. If you're interested in capitalizing on one of the hottest business trends on the Internet, give a call to my twenty-four-hour information hotline. . ." and so on. "It's something unique," says Jerry. "They won't throw it away."

CD-ROM Business Card

The ultimate business card is the so-called CD-ROM business card. It is a CD-ROM that can be played on any computer. But it is as small as a regular business card. Pop it into your laptop CD-ROM drive, and it plays a full-scale multimedia presentation of your product or opportunity. Video Plus in Lake Dallas, Texas, is one company that produces such cards.

Voice-Mail Business Card

Make up business cards that promote your product, service, or opportunity. The card should feature a twenty-four-hour hotline, preferably a toll-free 800 number that people can call to get more information (possibly with an offer of a free catalog, as a further inducement for people to call).

When people call the hotline, they get a voice-mail menu. If they press number one, they might get a three-minute recorded message giving them an overview of the business. If they press two, they might get a twenty- to thirty-minute live, pre-paid teleconference (see "Teleconferencing," further on). Number three might offer an explanation of the compensation plan. Number four could

> Voice-mail prospecting is a great time-saver. It helps you reach more people, since it is automated and you don't have to do all the explaining yourself.

send them to a Web site (see "Web Site Promotion," further on). Number five might tell them how to get started. Number six might present recorded testimonials from satisfied customers or successful distributors. Number seven might lead them to a fax-on-demand system (see Fax on Demand," further on).

Voice-mail prospecting is a great time-saver. It helps you reach more people, since it is automated and you don't have to do all the explaining yourself. Also, it pre-qualifies your prospects. Anyone who calls the 800 number, listens to the information, and then calls you back afterward is guaranteed to be seriously interested in the business. The tire-kickers will be screened out before you ever have to waste time with them.

Videotape

A great way to screen interested prospects is to ask them to view a promotional videotape. This can be a corporate video provided by your company that promotes your product or opportunity, or a generic video, such as those produced by Brilliant Compensation (www.brilliantcompensation.com), that promotes network marketing in general as a viable and potentially lucrative profession.

Ask your prospects whether they are interested in diversifying their income with a great part-time home-based business opportunity of their own. Next, ask them if the timing is right. In other words, are they ready to take action now, if the right opportunity comes along? If the answer to both these questions is yes, it's probably worthwhile to give them a videotape. Ask them to view it within a certain time period, say three days, at the end of which you will give them a call. If they view it, they're good prospects. If they keep making excuses for not viewing it, don't waste your time. They're not really interested.

Audiotape

Use the audiotape pretty much the same way you would use a videotape. The advantage of an audiotape is that many people have tape players in their cars. You can suggest that they listen to it while driving to work. This is easier for many people to do and requires less time commitment than watching a video at home.

Company Magazine

The chief disadvantage of an audiotape or videotape is that people have to expend effort in order to view or listen to it. They have to take it home, hang onto it until they're ready to view or listen to it, then finally pop it in the video or audio player and listen. A lot of opportunities will arise in between for prospects to simply lose the video or audio or forget about it.

A glossy company magazine, on the other hand, makes an instant impression. As soon as you place it in the prospects' hands, they see that it is attractive, slick, and professional-looking. This provides "third-party" validation. It shows prospects that you are not just an individual. You represent an organization that puts out an attractive magazine. Even if they never open it up, they have already gotten the impression that there is substance behind your sales pitch, and the impression sticks.

Many MLM companies publish monthly magazines or newsletters, with product and company information, as well as profiles of successful distributors. Always keep a supply on hand for your prospects. And remember to clip your business card to it.

Promotional Calendars

Many conventional businesses give out free calendars at the beginning of each year that contain advertisements for their business. Network marketers can use this tried-and-true promotional method as well. Look in the Yellow Pages under "specialty advertising" or go to any printshop. Make sure the calendar includes your name, phone number, and other contact information. People are less likely to discard an attractive calendar than other types of hand-outs.

FOLLOW-UP

After people respond to your sales aids or your verbal pitch, what do you do next? Follow-up is where the rubber meets the road in networking.

One-on-One Presentations

Ideally, you want to set up a one-on-one meeting with the prospect, where you present the opportunity. This meeting can be done in person or over the phone. The mere act of setting such an appointment tests your prospect's resolve, demonstrating whether he or she is committed enough to make and keep an appointment with you. It also gives you a chance to make an effective presentation. "The highest conversion ratio of all networking is where you can actually physically talk to a person," says Campisi. "In a one-on-one, you can develop rapport."

Two-on-One Presentations

If you are inexperienced, a two-on-one presentation may be more effective for you. That means bringing along your sponsor or upline to the meeting to make the presentation for you, while you watch and learn. As a leader, you want to encourage your recruits to use you for two-on-one presentations. But be careful lest they start using you as a crutch. Some leaders set limits on two-on-ones. They will offer to do three or four of them for each recruit, after which the recruit is on his own.

Three-Way Party Conferencing.

Commonly known as "three-way calling," this is a technological option that enables leaders to participate in two-on-one presentations more often and more efficiently. You can subscribe to a three-way conferencing service from your phone company. When one of your recruits needs you for a phone presentation, he rings you up, and you jump right into the call. You make the presentation to the prospect, while your recruit listens and learns. After three or four times, most recruits will have learned your selling technique sufficiently to do it themselves.

Teleconferencing

Another technological option used in network marketing is teleconferencing. As a leader, you announce that you are giving a sales presentation, via teleconference, at a particular time of the day or night. Many leaders hold regular teleconferences either once or several times a week. Distributors in your downline can then ask their recruits to phone in to the special conference line at the announced time and listen to the presentation. The presentations can be as simple or elaborate as you like. They can involve live testimonials from successful distributors, pep talks from various leaders in your downline, and even question-and-answer sessions in which conference participants can interact with the speakers. "With teleconferencing, you can totally leverage yourself," says Jerry. "You're handling not one or two individuals at a time, but you're talking to your whole group, around the country. You're helping your whole group expand at once."

Fax on Demand

During prospecting, networkers often feel that they are repeating themselves, like robots, saying the same things over and over to one prospect after another. Some of this is unavoidable, since every prospect does need to hear the same sales presentation and receive the same information about the product and opportunity. However, there are ways to alleviate the monotony through automation. One technique is fax on demand. This means setting up an automated fax line that your prospects can call, in order to obtain certain types of information. When they reach the line, they hear a voice menu offering them different categories of information, such as an executive summary of the business, a product overview, how to order products, how to sign up as a distributor, answers to frequently asked questions (FAQs), and so on. Whichever information they select, the service will then send it instantly to their fax machine. "Fax on demand is great," says Jerry. "You can actually set up your business around a fax on demand and say to the people, 'Listen, I have a very exciting business. I don't have time to tell you about it. Just call this fax on demand and you can pull down this information.'"

Web Page

Of course, the ultimate in automated prospecting is the interactive Web page. Instead of sending prospects to a fax-on-demand service, you can give them a business card with your URL or Web address and ask them to take a look at your Web page. Depending on how fancy you want to get, such pages can include full multimedia presentations of your business opportunity. They can include autoresponders that e-mail visitors automatically; interactive sign-up forms for new distributors; e-commerce functions for ordering products; announcements of upcoming events; downloading of information sheets; as well as links and instructions for accessing other information sources, such as fax on demand or voice mail.

> Instead of sending prospects to a fax-on-demand service, you can give them a business card with your URL or Web address and ask them to take a look at your Web page.

Many companies place tight restrictions on the use of Web pages by distributors, and some forbid it altogether. That is because companies can be held legally responsible for any inaccurate or misleading information posted online by individual distributors. Some companies solve this problem by providing their own in-house Web hosting service, in which distributors sign up for a cookie-cutter Web page whose content is tightly controlled by the head office. Always find out your company's policy before taking your marketing efforts online.

One way to use Web follow-up without the complications of posting your own Web page is to send prospects to generic Web sites that promote network marketing as an industry. Such Web sites do not market your particular company, of course, and cannot provide automated sign-up and e-commerce functions for your business. But they do help you deal with the number one most-asked question from all MLM prospects: "Is MLM a legitimate business or is it a pyramid scheme?" An excellent generic MLM online presentation can be found at: www.brilliantcompensation.com. (Jerry's favorite generic online training and lead generation site is www.nmonline.net.)

Weekly Business Meeting

A tried-and-true method of follow-up in network marketing is to invite prospects to attend a "business briefing" or "opportunity meeting." These meetings are typically held in rented hotel conference rooms. Sometimes they are staid, business-like affairs. Other times they resemble football pep rallies or revival-tent meetings. The style varies from company to company and from leader to leader. But what they all have in common is providing a regular event—usually weekly, but sometimes more than once a week—to which everyone in your downline can invite prospects.

At the meeting, a keynote speaker—generally, the leader who is sponsoring the meeting—will give a talk in which he or she presents and promotes the business opportunity. There may be product demonstrations. There may be testimonials from successful distributors. But the main action happens after the speeches are over, when everyone breaks up into groups or circulates around the room, talking to guests and trying to persuade them to sign up.

Opportunity meetings have long been the primary vehicle of MLM prospecting. They offer tremendous leverage for a leader, who can reach hundreds of people at a time through these meetings, and are also a great sales aid for distributors, who can bring their prospects to the event and allow the speakers and the excitement of the event to do much of their prospecting for them.

Jerry cautions, however, that business meetings can become a crutch to one's downline. If you use weekly meetings, be wary of allowing your people to depend on them too much. Make sure that they are working the business in other ways as well and not just spending the whole week inviting people to the meeting.

"It is very important that you do not have your whole organization do the business only once a week," says Jerry. "The meeting is done to provide synergy, but your downline should also be doing one-on-ones and talking to people on the telephone. If they rely on bringing people to the meeting once a week, then they're only going to do the business four times a month. They should be doing all the other techniques at the same time. That's a big lesson to learn in this business. People tend to lean on other people to do the business for them, when they should be stepping up to leadership and doing other techniques on their own."

In-Home Meetings

Many networkers today prefer to avoid hotel meetings for two reasons. First, the cost of hotel conference room rentals has skyrocketed in recent years. Second, because many people work longer hours today, and because both husband and wife are often working, people are less inclined to give up whatever precious free time they may have in the evening to pile into their car during a rain or snowstorm and drive off to the local Ramada Inn.

One increasingly popular compromise is the in-home meeting. This is a smaller, more informal version of the hotel meeting that takes place right in your living room. There you can play a videotape, walk your guests through an on-line presentation, or give a product demonstration.

Speakerphone Conferencing

As a leader, you cannot be personally present at every in-home meeting given by your downline. But you can *participate* personally in many different meetings, through the technique of speakerphone conferencing. Simply instruct your downline leaders to invite people to in-home meetings. After their guests view the video, the hosts can inform them that they will have the chance to interact with so-and-so, an experienced and successful sales leader in the company. That's where you step in, as the leader. You address the group from a remote location via speakerphone and do a ten- to fifteen-minute presentation. This technique enables leaders to participate personally in meetings all across the country, and even internationally, without being physically present.

Satellite Conferencing

Some companies offer private satellite television programming that includes televised training and opportunity meetings featuring the company president and top sales leaders. You can invite guests for an in-home meeting when these programs are being broadcast and make the satellite program the focus of your presentation.

> Some companies offer private satellite television programming that includes televised training and opportunity meetings featuring the company president and top sales leaders.

Professional Business Letter

You can find many different ways to invite people to meetings, both formal and informal, depending on your personal style, the style of the meeting, and the nature of that particular contact. One formal way to present the invitation is by means of a business letter on professional stationery.

Professional Business Postcard

You can also print up standardized business letters on oversized postcards that promote your product or opportunity. Or you can print up standardized postcards and fasten a more personalized business letter to them. These can be mailed out to your prospects.

Invitations, Formal or Informal

You can print up postcards or flyers specifically worded as an invitation to your weekly meetings, in-home gatherings, or other events. They can be more or less formal, depending on the style of the event. "These can double your response rate," says Jerry. "You get much more response if you give someone an invitation in writing. People tend to forget, but now they have something physical to remind them."

Multimedia Info Kit

It is often effective to send people a multimedia kit that includes both audio- and videotape, along with printed material promoting your opportunity. These kits are expensive and should only be sent as a follow-up to prospects who have already expressed an interest. Some distributors charge the prospect five or ten dollars for the kit, offering to send it out COD. If the prospect decides he is not interested, he sends the materials back and his money is refunded.

ONLINE MARKETING

Web Site Promotion

As noted earlier, many companies discourage individual distributors from promoting the business via a Web site, except through company-approved, pre-formatted sites. Even if your company allows Web site promotion, this is not a magic bullet. The sheer number of Web sites on the Internet—which is multiplying every month—means that your Web site is fighting an ever-more-difficult battle to distinguish itself from all the other Web sites out there.

Unless they have seen your site advertised somewhere, people will not be able to find it, except by chance, through a search engine. They might have heard of your company, for instance. If they go to a search engine like google.com or mamma.com, and type in the name of your company, your Web site may come out near the top of the list or it may appear as number 200 on the list. The same applies if they type in another type of search word related to the sort of product you are selling. You can try to stay at the top of these search lists by constantly updating your registration with the various search engines, but thousands of other people are doing the same thing.

The bottom line is that Web sites are not an effective promotional device in and of themselves. They are more effective as an adjunct to other marketing methods, such as passing out business cards or flyers with your Web address on them. However, techniques exist for increasing Web traffic that the committed online networker may wish to pursue. For a wealth of suggestions along these lines, Jerry recommends the book *Increase Your Web Traffic in a Weekend* by William Robert Stanek, which is available through Amazon.com.

Chat Rooms and Message Boards

One way to steer people toward your site is to participate in online discussions, via chat room and message board, pertaining either to network marketing in general or to subjects related to your particular product or service. When you find people who seem interested in what you have to say, you can exchange e-mails with them and recommend that they visit your Web site.

E-Zines

Another effective method of Internet promotion is to publish a periodical e-mail magazine, called an e-zine. The trick here, as with offering seminars, is to provide useful information. An advertising pitch disguised as an e-zine will fool no one and will only annoy most recipients. But if you can provide truly useful and helpful information on your chosen subject, people will look forward to your e-mailings and will be more open to finding out about your opportunity.

A word of caution is in order here. Internet people take a dim view of "spam"—a derogatory word for unsolicited e-mail promotions. In some cases, angry recipients of such promotions may report them to the appropriate Internet Service Provider (ISP) and get the sender kicked off the service.

Some spammers send messages that say something like: "This is not spam. You are receiving this e-mail newsletter because you have previously requested or subscribed to it. If you do not wish to receive it, see below for instructions to unsubscribe . . . ," etc.

Personally, I find such messages annoying. When a salesman tells me that I have subscribed to something that I know I have never subscribed to, he is insulting my intelligence. Instead of building a bond with me, which is a salesman's goal, he is antagonizing me. This is no way to make a sale. I would not recommend this method to anyone, unless, of course, your goal is to irritate your prospects.

A variety of techniques are available for marketing e-zines and other commercial e-mail messages that do not put you afoul of laws, regulations, or people's feelings, and these can be found in many books about Internet marketing, available through Amazon.com.

STRATEGIC ALLIANCES

One way to leverage your marketing efforts is by making strategic alliances with other businesspeople and gaining access to their customer bases. You can get them to help you market your product or business by offering them a 50 percent cut of your profits each time they help you get a product order or a recruit. Many MLM companies can track these sorts of transactions for you through their computerized accounting systems, so you don't have to tabulate them yourself.

These alliances serve a twofold purpose. First, they give you access to leads that you would not otherwise get. Second, they give you a way to recruit other businesspeople into your downline. In most cases, says Jerry, if a businessman agrees to work with you as a strategic partner, he will soon realize that it is more profitable for him to work as a member of your downline. "Instead of making 50 percent of your profits, they can make 100 percent of whatever the profits are for that particular business, by signing up and becoming a distributor," he says. Following are a number of techniques for employing strategic partners in your business.

> One way to leverage your marketing efforts is by making strategic alliances with other businesspeople and gaining access to their customer bases.

Referral Agents

Sometimes interested prospects will say they do not have enough money to enroll in the business as regular distributors.

In such cases, you can propose that they become referral agents for you. All they have to do is refer customers and potential recruits to you, and you will give them 50 percent of your profits for any transactions that result from their referrals.

"Some distributors have ten or twenty referral agents, and they come home from work, and there are leads all over the place," says Jerry. "Then as soon as your referral agents have enough money to sign in properly, you can sign them in."

Jerry points out that the referral agent technique is an effective objection-handling technique. The fact is that the entry cost of an MLM business is generally so low that most people can afford it if they really want. But many people, because they have not yet crossed the psychological bridge of wanting to sign up as a distributor, will offer the excuse that "It costs too much" as a way of buying time and delaying their decision. Offering such people the option of becoming a referral agent bypasses this objection, presents them with a no-risk opportunity to make money, and brings them one step closer to making a final decision.

"Once you offer people that opportunity, many of them will say, 'Well, let me just sign in as a distributor,'" says Jerry. "You can use this technique to find out whether they're really interested or not."

Patron Partner Program

A variant of the referral agent technique is the patron partner program. Here, you offer discount coupons on product purchases in exchange for referrals. You say to the prospect, "For every three leads you give me, I'll give you X percent off on your next purchase."

The exact amount of the discount depends on how your particular marketing plan is structured. But let's say you'll give him 20 percent off, in exchange for three referrals. That means if he gives you fifteen referrals (three times five), he gets 100 percent off. In other words, he gets his next product order free of charge. That is a strong inducement for many prospects to send you leads. "If you give every customer the opportunity to get his or her product free by giving you so many referrals, you will have a system providing an endless supply of leads," says Jerry.

Brochure Holders with Product Cards

You can make deals with various types of retailers to place brochures with free promotional information in their establishments. Some MLM companies provide these "take-one-free" plastic or cardboard brochure holders as a service to distributors. If your company does not, you can easily have them made up. Before you do, find out your company's policy on such promotions, as some MLM companies restrict or forbid the use of them.

Look for high-traffic locations that attract upscale customers with a special interest in your product or service, such as a dry cleaner, a health club, a natural food store, or a computer store. Then approach the proprietors of those businesses and tell them that if they permit you to place your brochure holder near their cash registers, you will pay them 50 percent of your profits on any leads who come through their business. The proprietors may either agree to these terms or decide that it is more profitable to sign up as distributors in your downline and receive 100 percent of the profits from the leads generated by your brochure holder. Either way, you're a winner.

Business and Franchise Show Prospecting

Business opportunity and franchise shows are an ideal hunting ground for network marketers, because people attend those shows for the specific purpose of bettering their lives by getting into business. Check with your company first, as some MLM firms do not allow distributors to recruit at such shows.

Whether your company allows such recruiting or not, you can always gain access to attendees by cutting a deal with the salesmen who represent the various franchises and business opportunities. These salesmen make excellent recruits and referral agents for you, because they travel around the country, meeting highly qualified people with a serious interest in entrepreneurship. Many of the leads they get are not right for the type of business they are offering, perhaps because they don't have the money to buy a franchise. But these same leads could be perfect for an MLM opportunity.

"Tell them, 'Look, you're getting leads that you don't use,'" says Jerry. "'I would love to take a shot at those leads. At no cost to you, I'll give you 50 percent of the profits I earn from those leads.'" Jerry reports that many franchise and business opportunity salesmen are intrigued by this proposal and readily agree to it. Before entering into such an arrangement, however, make sure that the deal does not violate any pre-existing contracts to which the representatives may have agreed.

Lead Exchange

You can also exchange leads with businesses that might have customers suitable for cross-marketing between your business and theirs. Let's say you are selling a health-related product. You might propose a lead exchange with a health club or wellness center. "You could say, 'Look, your customers want to improve their health,'" suggests Jerry, "'and I'm interested in selling a health-related product that you don't market. Why don't we exchange? Everyone I get who's interested in my health-related business, I'll give you the leads, and with your people who subscribe to your health club, if you allow me to market to them, I'll give you 50 percent of the profits I earn from them. There's nothing to lose, and the bottom line to gain for the health club.' Many business owners find that proposition attractive," says Jerry.

Banner Ads on the Net

Many Web sites fail to make money, despite high levels of traffic. Owners of such sites are often wide open for suggestions on how to turn their traffic into profit. Jerry recommends offering them a deal. Tell them if they post your ad banner promoting your MLM business, you'll give them 50 percent of the profits from every prospect who clicks through that ad and ends up doing business with you, as a customer or distributor. Since the banner ad costs the Web site nothing, it is an attractive proposition. And, of course, if the Web site owner chooses to become a full-fledged distributor in your business, he can take 100 percent of the profits from the business it reaps. Either way, you pay nothing to place the ad on his high-traffic Web site.

Discount Offers on Receipts

Many businesses now put advertising on the back of receipts. Network marketers can use this space to make product discount offers. Find businesses whose customers are likely to have an interest in your product or service. Tell the proprietors that if they let you put your discount coupon on the back of their receipts, you'll give them 50 percent of the profits generated from their leads. Of course, you will be dependent on the prospects themselves to call you. You will not be able to get any information on them. But the fact that you are offering a product discount will induce many to pick up the phone. "This is an inexpensive way of getting new leads," says Jerry. "Every day you can come back from work and have leads."

TOP DOWN, BOTTOM UP, INSIDE OUT

At the heart of Jerry's training program is the recognition that there are three ways of working a network marketing business. Jerry calls them: Top Down, Bottom Up, and Inside Out.

Top Down

This means recruiting distributors first and allowing those distributors to get customers for you. Your own personal recruiting efforts are focused on finding business builders, leaders who are likely to become powerful recruiters in their own right. Many leaders in networking strive to build from the top down, because it leads to rapid growth. But it also creates problems. The leaders you recruit will tend to train their people just the way you trained them. They will follow your example. And if everyone in your downline is looking for business builders and leaders, then no one is looking for customers. You get a lot of recruiting activity without many product sales.

Bottom Up

This means finding customers first, then recruiting leaders from among your customers. The main thrust of your selling is to interest people in the product or service rather than in the business opportunity. It takes a little longer to build a network marketing business this way. But it will give you a much more solid organization, based upon product sales to end users. "Remember, one of the best distributors you can get is a committed product user," says Jerry. "A lot of times, networkers go strictly after distributors. They don't realize that customers turn into distributors. If you have 1,000 distributors and each has 20 customers, then you have 20,000 retail customers. It depends on what you teach. If you don't teach techniques for getting customers, then the people in your downline won't do it."

Inside Out

Jerry recommends combining both techniques. He calls his method "Inside Out" marketing. "You start from the inside of the person, getting inside him emotionally," says Jerry. You do this by providing *service*. First, you win the person over as a customer, by selling him your product or service. Then you overwhelm him with customer service.

"The days of just signing up customers and saying thank you very much are gone," says Jerry. "In the 2000s, whoever can touch the customer most, whoever will service him most, will keep him. Through the Internet, you can touch that customer every day. If you're not on the Internet, you can still touch him or her by picking up the phone. You can send thank-you cards. When was the last time you went to a store and the salesperson called you up and thanked you for the sale? You do that, and customers will never leave you. You'll get that person from the inside." From the dedicated customer base you create through service, you can then begin cherry-picking, singling out the best, most ambitious prospects and offering them the business opportunity.

> First, you win the person over as a customer, by selling him your product or service. Then you overwhelm him with customer service.

In keeping with the 80/20 Rule discussed in part 1, Jerry predicts that networkers should be able to glean about two leaders from every ten good, steady customers they retain.

THE PRODUCT APPROACH

The key to winning customers, of course, is to sell them the product or service. A number of tried-and-true techniques can help you do this:

Basket Pass Out

This is derived from the traditional "puppy-dog" sales technique. The way to sell a puppy is to let people hold it and play with it. Once they've done that, they will not be able to resist buying the puppy.

"If you can get your customer to physically try a product, your sale, your conversion rate is much higher," says Jerry. "This is why when you go into chain supermarkets nowadays, they're trying to feed you food as you walk in the door. They know that if you try that food, there's a good chance that some of you will go over and buy that item right then."

One way to put that principle to work in your networking business is to give prospects a basket of free samples, attractively designed and presented. This method works best with consumables, such as personal care products or nutritional supplements. Tell your prospect, "These are free samples. I'll give them to you on the condition that you promise me you'll try them for a week. Now, you can keep the products, but I need the basket back. I'll come to pick it up at the end of the week, and I'm going to see how many products you've used."

"This is a very effective method," Jerry comments. "You'd be surprised at the conversion rate." Once people have actually used and like the products, they are far more inclined to buy refills.

Holiday Specials

Traditional retailers always run specials on holidays, when people have more leisure to buy things. Network marketers can do the same. Plan in advance, and notify your prospects through all the usual MLM methods (many described in this chapter) that you will be offering special discounts during the upcoming holiday.

Gift Certificates

Another method that networkers can borrow from traditional retailing is the use of gift certificates. It is very effective for getting people to try your products and services, because people feel obligated to use something a friend or family member has given them. Some MLM companies provide gift certificates as a standard service to their distributors. But if your company doesn't, you can always design your own and produce them at a local print shop.

Give Out Samples at Special Events

Many special events, such as summer fairs, car shows, and the like, provide an ideal place to pass out free samples. You may need permission from the promoter, but this is usually not a problem. It is especially effective to target events that relate to your type of product or service: computer shows if you are selling Internet service; health fairs if you are selling nutritional products; and so on.

Product Roundtables

This is a variation on the hotel meeting, described earlier, except that it focuses on moving product rather than recruiting distributors. Such events can be held at lunchtime or during the evening. You rent a hotel conference room and fill it with large round tables capable of seating 10 to 15 people apiece. The cost is split between leaders in your downline who participate in the event. For instance, if the room costs $300 to rent and you have 30 roundtables, then the cost of each table is $10. Leaders in your downline will rent the tables in advance and be responsible for filling their respective tables with people.

Jerry advises having a host and hostess at each table, to market more effectively to both men and women. The samples are displayed on the table. "Let people feel, touch, smell," Jerry suggests. "The more senses that you use in a presentation, the higher the closing ratio. These are very effective for selling lots and lots of product."

No networking is done at product roundtables. The focus is strictly on selling products and services. However, you should pass out flyers saying that distributorships are available and that interested people should ask the person who invited them about it. That way, no one who is interested in the opportunity will fall through the cracks.

In-Home Product Clinics

This is the product version of the in-home opportunity meeting. Invite people to your home, just as you would for a satellite or speakerphone meeting, but focus on presenting and selling the product or service rather than on the business opportunity.

Product Seminars at Nursing and Retirement Homes

Retirement homes maintain programs of activities for the entertainment and benefit of their clients. Talk to the events coordinator at the home and get permission to do a product seminar. Generally, you will be welcome as long as you present your product or service in an informal, educational way, without heavy selling.

Sample Card Pass Out

When you give out free samples, it is a good idea to fasten a card onto them with a brief explanation of the product and of course, contact information should the customer wish to get in touch with you later. The card can also feature your Web site address, voice-mail number, fax-on-demand service, or other follow-up options.

Product Card Pass Out

You can also pass out product cards without a sample attached, simply to spur the curiosity of potential customers who may not be ready to buy yet.

Product Catalog Pass Out

Most MLM companies offer an attractively produced catalog of their products and services. These glossy publications make a strong impression on prospects and potential customers and can be handed out to build interest in the products. Be sure to attach your business card or other contact information to each catalog.

THE ULTIMATE LEVERAGE

Jerry emphasizes that the ideas presented in this chapter— and in his training seminars—are in no way definitive. Their purpose is not to present distributors with an encyclopedia of every known method of network marketing. Indeed, plenty more are in Jerry's arsenal beyond those presented here. Moreover, it is important to remember that laws and regulations governing particular MLM techniques vary from company to company and state to state, so network marketers—like all businesspeople—must make a point of familiarizing themselves with the rules of the game before adopting any particular techniques. (A good place to start is to ask your upline.) The point of this chapter, however is that if you can seed your distributors' brains with ideas, they will soon begin inventing strategies of their own. Then you will gain the ultimate leverage, benefiting not only from many peoples' efforts but from their minds as well.

CHAPTER 17

Strategy Number 3— Lead by Persuasion

One of the most interesting leadership books I ever read was written not by an executive, consultant, or entrepreneur but by a former cop. It was called *Verbal Judo: The Gentle Art of Persuasion,* by George Thompson with Jerry Jenkins. An accomplished martial artist, as well as a former English professor, Thompson brought a unique perspective to his job of street cop. His education and martial arts background—unusual for a rank-and-file policeman—enabled him to make penetrating observations about the challenges officers face every day and the techniques they use for overcoming them.

Thompson discovered that many suspects, when confronted by a cop, are openly defiant. They will refuse an outright command and challenge you to do something about it. Thompson, a two-hundred-pound bruiser with an evil temper, found that his first impulse was to meet such challenges with physical force. He would yank the suspect from the car, rough him up, and slap on the cuffs without a moment's hesitation. But soon, complaints of Thompson's "brutality" began piling up. A veteran cop advised Thompson to use less force and more "persuasion."

Easier Said Than Done

Any salesman who has ever sat through a customer-service seminar knows how Officer Thompson felt at that moment. It is easy to say, "The customer is always right." But it is far harder to remember that principle when you are under verbal attack from some irate customer. Likewise, it seemed easy for that veteran cop to say, "Use persuasion." But things were different out on the street. Or so Thompson believed.

Most people respond with their jungle instincts when under attack. But that is not the way to get results. Great leaders seldom show anger or belligerence to the people they lead. No matter what the provocation, they strive to meet each attack or insult with calmness and detachment.

Leaders develop practical skills for disengaging themselves from their emotions. According to Donald Phillips in *Lincoln on Leadership,* Abraham Lincoln used to compose angry letters to people who had offended him, then seal those letters in an envelope and put them away. He would never send them. The next time he dealt with that person, his anger would have dissipated. But because he had not sent the letter, the relationship was still intact.

> Leaders develop practical skills for disengaging themselves from their emotions.

Verbal Judo

Officer Thompson faced a similar challenge in his job. How could he "persuade" a belligerent suspect to do what he wanted, when every muscle in his body was itching to grab that suspect by the collar and throw him against the car?

As a cop, Thompson had learned that the wrong words uttered in a tense moment can lead to disaster or death. But the right ones can resolve a situation safely and satisfactorily. The key to knowing what to say turned out to be a principle that Thompson had learned in martial arts. He called it "verbal judo."

DETACHMENT

The first step in mastering verbal judo was to achieve self-control. The ancient samurai called this *mushin*—a detached state of mind in which you study your opponent and redirect his aggression in the midst of combat. Thompson discovered several tricks for inducing *mushin* in the heat of confrontation.

Technique Number 1

Train yourself to welcome conflict. Look forward to such tests as the samurai anticipated combat. For a samurai, the issue isn't winning or losing, living or dying, but "bravely engaging, fighting with great style, learning from the encounter."

Technique Number 2

Use active listening. This means paraphrasing what somebody says back to you. Many communication experts recommend this technique as a way to clarify what you just heard. But it can also defuse a volatile situation. Suppose a suspect is pouring out a stream of angry invective at Officer Thompson. To interrupt would only make the suspect angrier. But Thompson discovered that most people will tolerate one type of interruption. You say, "Let me be sure I heard what you just said." Then paraphrase it back to him. Just about anyone will sit still to hear his own position stated. But now *you're* doing the talking, and *he's* listening! You've already turned the tables on him, without raising your voice.

Technique Number 3

Use strip phrases. Thompson learned that when a street punk cursed him out, he could check his anger by using abbreviated, slightly distorted phrases to "strip" the insult of its power. He'd say, "*I 'preciate that,* sir (instead of 'appreciate'), but I still need to see some I.D.*" Or, "I *understan'* that, sir" (instead of "I understand"). Somehow, the tiny effort involved in using the distorted "strip phrase" calmed Thompson and made him appreciate the chess-like tactics of the moment. It also injected humor into the situation. Only Thompson knew that he was deliberately mispronouncing words. It was like playing a private little joke on the suspect. And it worked! The exercise helped Thompson stay calm.

Technique Number 4

Name your enemy. As a boy, Thompson had befriended an American Indian man who used to impart traditional wisdom to him. His Indian friend once told Thompson that the first step to defeating your enemy is to call him by his proper name. Thompson put this principle to work in formulating his "verbal judo" techniques. When suspects challenged Thompson by saying, "I don't have to do that!" or "You have no right to . . ." a little voice inside him responded, "Wanna bet?" Thompson realized that this little voice was his enemy. It was a force that provoked him to overreact. Thompson decided to give that voice a name. He called it the "Wanna Bet Guy." The mere act of naming it helped Thompson recognize and avoid the pugnacious spirit whenever it threatened to undermine his professionalism.

OFFER A CHOICE

Once he had achieved *mushin* or self-control, Thompson discovered that his anger no longer clouded his judgment. It became easier to find solutions. For instance, if a suspect refused to hand over his I.D., Thompson would say something like, "I understan' that, sir, so let me give you a choice. You can show me some I.D., and then I can let you go on your way, or I can put you under arrest right now, and take you down to the station." A choice like that gets people's attention. And if it is offered in a spirit of detached self-control, it reassures and calms your opponent, even while putting pressure on him. Officer Thompson became a good cop through the application of *mushin*.

PERSUASION

Mushin is just as vital for MLM leaders as it is for street cops and samurai swordsmen. Network marketers deal constantly with frustration: prospects who make appointments, then don't show up; friends and relatives who attack your business as a pyramid scam; people in your downline who complain and criticize, break promises, and don't follow through. A dedicated, hard-driving leader might be tempted, in such situations, to behave like Officer Thompson and just start slamming people around (metaphorically speaking, of course).

> MLM leaders need to master the art of "persuasion" in order to get what they want.

But that doesn't work in MLM any better than it does in police work. Like Officer Thompson, MLM leaders need to master the art of "persuasion" in order to get what they want.

THE THREE STEPS TO PERSUASIVE DOWNLINE-BUILDING

In chapter 12, we met Cindy Samuelson, the feisty Filipina immigrant with the take-no-prisoners leadership style. Her turning point came when a crossline leader named Bob Schmidt agreed to teach her the secrets of noninvasive selling. They were:

Step 1

Detachment. Let go of your intense desire to close a sale.

Step 2

Nonconfrontational selling. Give your prospects room and respect their space, so they can make an informed decision in peace and with dignity.

Step 3

Building in depth. Deepen your downline constantly, so that you spread out your risk and do not place all your hopes in a few frontline people.

In the pages that follow, we will explore how Cindy put those principles to work in her business.

The "Perfect" Sales Call

As described in chapter 12, Cindy approached Bob after he came to speak in her hometown of Phoenix, Arizona. She asked him to spend a day making sales calls with her, to critique her selling style.

Cindy had a trick up her sleeve. She had lined up a perfect prospect, a successful businessman—head of a national collection agency—who seemed interested in her opportunity and whom Cindy was sure she could close that day. It was a perfect set-up to impress Bob with her selling skill.

But Cindy's plan fell flat. She and Bob had lunch with the man. Cindy turned on the charm, using every technique she knew to relax her prospect, then build rapport with him and finally move in for the kill and get him to close. Despite her efforts, the man proved immovable. He refused point-blank to join her business. The lunch ended in failure, and Cindy was at a loss to explain it.

THE SANDWICH TECHNIQUE

Bob saw the problem clearly, though. After the meeting, he took Cindy aside. "You were absolutely stunning," he began. "Your presentation was great. You made him feel comfortable. And then at the end, it fell apart. You pounded him into submission. You were unmerciful. And that's why you lost the sale."

Bob was himself using a time-honored persuasion strategy on Cindy. Mary Kay Ash, the founder and chairman of Mary Kay Cosmetics, had named this strategy "the Sandwich Technique." Whenever you need to criticize one of your people, Mary Kay teaches, you take that person aside for a private conversation. Then you think of two things that person does well. Begin the conversation by praising him for something he did right. That is the first slice of bread. Then tell him what he did wrong. That's the meat. Finally, you end the meeting by praising something else he did well. That's the final slice of bread. Sandwiching criticism between two slices of praise takes the edge off it and lowers the person's defenses.

GIVE THEM SPACE

After complimenting her for what she did right, Bob got down to business. He analyzed Cindy's sales approach and showed her where she went wrong. Her worst mistake, Bob said, was to use aggressive closing tactics. Cindy had learned these tactics in traditional selling jobs. She had learned that you never expect to get the order the first time you ask for it. So you ask many times. And each time the prospect raises an objection, you shoot down the objection and ask again, so that your prospect is backed into a corner.

That's what Cindy had done with this businessman. "I pushed and pushed," she recalls. First she offered the product. "Are you ready to buy now?" she would ask. "Why aren't you ready to buy now? Why isn't the timing right now?" Then she pressed him on joining her downline. "Are you ready to join my team today?" she asked. "Well, why not? I've answered that objection, so why can't you make a decision now?" All Cindy's pushing got her nowhere. The more she pushed, the more her prospect pushed back. Finally, he excused himself and ended the luncheon.

Small-Time Tactics, Big-Time Sale

Without realizing it, Cindy had treated her prospect with disdain. She had failed to acknowledge the importance of the decision she was asking him to make. In the process, she had also insulted her prospect's intelligence. He was sophisticated enough to know that joining Cindy's downline was a big decision that should not be made rashly. By pushing him so hard, Cindy was, in effect, urging him to take imprudent action.

Network marketers are not the only people who make this mistake. All salesmen struggle with the temptation to employ small-time closing tactics when they make big-time sales. Sales consultant Neil Rackham of Huthwaite, Inc., has analyzed this phenomenon for years. He discovered that inappropriate closing tactics are one of the chief reasons for sales failure today.

Heavy Risk

After analyzing more than 35,000 transactions over a ten-year period, Rackham discovered that there are fundamental differences between small sales and large ones. In a small sale, such as for women's shoes, the traditional tactics of probing, objection-handling, and closing work fine. But these same tactics will blow up in your face if you try to apply them to a buyer for a large corporation.

Rackham explains why in his book *SPIN Selling*. It is a matter of risk. If you're selling a pair of women's shoes, your customer runs only a slight risk. She might decide after buying them that the shoes are not right for her. But that's all right. She has done the same thing many times before, as the pile of shoes gathering dust in her closet attests. So when a salesman pressures her to close, her inclination is to say, "Why not?"

It is far different with a company executive. If the computer system you are selling him turns out to be a lemon, he is in hot water with his boss. He will be blamed for misspending a large amount of money. Every time the system crashes or malfunctions, his name will come up. Large sales of this nature usually come with long-term service contracts. If the service is poor, the company risks being locked into a troublesome contract for years. Your hapless corporate buyer may end up losing his job over this disastrous transaction.

Skillful Questioning

Shooting down objections and pressing for a quick sale will not work in this situation. If you use high-pressure tactics, the buyer will think you are taking him for an idiot. And he will be right.

A more professional approach is to acknowledge that the risks your prospect faces are real. Don't try to dismiss them or talk them away. Instead, use his fears to your advantage. Convince your prospect that his risks will be greater if he fails to buy your product than if he buys it. This is accomplished through skillful, patient questioning. The trick is to get the prospect himself to acknowledge that he is in trouble and that your opportunity might be the way out for him. Neil Rackham recommends a four-step process for accomplishing this. His process has enabled several Fortune 500 clients to increase sales by 27 to 76 percent, in test campaigns. It is called "SPIN selling," which stands for *situation; problem; implication; need*. The steps are as follows:

Step 1: Situation

Get the facts on your prospect's situation. In network marketing, this can mean finding out what he does for a living, what level of income he makes, how many children he has, and so on. You must be sparing with these background questions, as they can easily tax your prospect's patience.

Step 2: Problem

Once you have the background, start probing for the problems. What are the challenges your prospect faces in his life, in his business? Does he have enough money? Enough free time? Does he worry whether he'll save enough for retirement?

Step 3: Implication

Once you know what your prospect perceives his problems to be, you can ask further questions that will help him see the implications of those problems. For instance, if his income is insufficient now, this implies that he will be in even worse trouble later if he gets sick, if he gets laid off, or when his kids enter college. As always, let your prospect arrive at the realization himself. Ask him questions that will help him think it through.

Step 4: Need

When your prospect has fully grasped the challenges facing him, ask him additional questions that will help him to see your opportunity as a possible solution. You goal is to get him to perceive a need for your opportunity. You want him to see that failing to try your opportunity may be a riskier course of action than trying it.

GIVE HIM SPACE

Selling high-ticket items is a long-term process. You should not attempt to close the deal in a single meeting. In fact, tell your prospect that this is a big decision and you do not want him to decide now. He must do his homework first. The key is follow-up. Stay in touch with the prospect periodically, and make yourself available to answer questions and help him get information. But do not press him to close.

MLM PROSPECTS ARE "BIG" CUSTOMERS

Bob Schmidt did not tell Cindy specifically about SPIN selling. But many of the principles he imparted to her were similar to those in Rackham's book. The techniques that are effective in recruiting network marketers greatly resemble those used in big corporate sales. That is because MLM prospects are in a similar position to that of a major corporate buyer.

Like a corporate executive faced with a major purchase, your MLM prospect is being asked to commit to a long-term relationship. When he signs on the dotted line, he risks money, time, labor, and status. Friends, family, and colleagues may taunt him for his choice. The company he is joining may run into financial problems ahead. Heavy sales pressure will only convince him that you are not taking his risks seriously.

LETTING GO

For Cindy, the first step in embracing this new sales philosophy was to acquire *mushin*. This was difficult for her, because she was overwhelmed by her intense desire to close a sale. "I wanted the money too badly," she recalls. "It's all I could think about."

A friend of Cindy's helped her work through this. He was a successful businessman in his seventies, with an eight-figure income. This friend asked Cindy what she would do if one day she had all the money she craved but still found she was coming up empty emotionally. The question frightened Cindy. "How many diamond rings and expensive cars could I buy? What would inspire me when I had all the money, and my fascination with jewelry was gone?"

He taught Cindy that what mattered was not making money but getting the job done and getting it done right. He got her to focus on the process rather than the result. This simple shift in perspective proved to be the catalyst that Cindy needed to achieve *mushin*—the sublime state of detachment necessary for a warrior. "It allowed me to become detached from the results," says Cindy. "I saw that it wasn't about making money. It was about transforming people's lives."

BUILDING IN DEPTH

Now Cindy had taken the first two steps in Bob's three-step process. She had *detached* herself from the desire to close and had begun practicing *noninvasive selling.* The next step was to *build in depth.*

Technically, building in depth simply means building an organization many levels deep. It is the obvious goal of any network marketer. In the ideal MLM organization, where you recruit five people and each of those five people recruit five people, and so on, the more levels you go down, the more people will be on each level. So it is at the very lowest levels of your pay range that the power of geometric progression will kick in. There you will find the most people, the most recruiting activity, and the most money being generated.

> **B**uilding in depth simply means building an organization many levels deep. It is the obvious goal of any network marketer.

NETWORK WITHIN YOUR NETWORK

The problem is that in a real MLM organization, as opposed to an ideal one, downlines tend to stay rather shallow unless you give them extra help. Most of the people you recruit will not automatically go out and recruit more people, nor will their recruits or the recruits of their recruits. Successful MLM leaders have learned to intervene personally in their lower levels, in order to ensure that their organizations keep growing.

This means networking within your network. Many networkers believe they have it made once they recruit an energetic and talented leader. But wise networkers don't just leave it at that. They go out of their way to form relationships with people further down the chain of command, to work with them directly and help them grow their organizations.

EVERYONE IS REPLACEABLE

Everyone must be replaceable in a healthy MLM downline. If you have invested too much of your time, energy, and hope in a particular leader, you may be in for a keen disappointment. Things happen. Leaders leave to join other companies or start their own companies. They retire from the business. They get sick or even die. They get divorced and start fighting with their ex-spouses over the business. And so on.

For a dozen different reasons, an otherwise thriving downline can suddenly atrophy or break up because of trouble with the leader at the top. But if you have reached out to people in the lower levels and formed direct relationships with them, you can salvage many good people from such disasters. Just because you lose a leader doesn't mean you have to lose his or her whole organization.

THE POWER OF RELATIONSHIPS

Building in depth is not so much a strategy as a mindset. It comes naturally, through the process of detachment. Inexperienced networkers look for an instant payoff. If they meet with a prospect, they want to close. If they recruit a distributor, they want him to build a productive downline. But seasoned networkers have learned to value relationships in and of themselves.

Every relationship can help your business. But the payoff may not be immediate. Sometimes the whole point of meeting someone may be so that person can lead you to another person who leads you to another person. Cindy cultivates relationships now without any clear idea of where those relationships will lead.

EXPAND YOUR NETWORK

The businessman who turned her down in that long-ago lunch meeting is still Cindy's friend. But to this day, he has never shown any inclination to join her downline. "I have never asked him for an order since that meeting," she says. "I never ask anybody for an order anymore. I just see each person as a tremendous asset for me, someone who can help me expand my reach, my network. One person may not be right for my business, but he may know someone marvelous who might be right for it."

FOLLOW-UP

The key is follow-up. Instead of pressing your prospect to make a decision, just stay available to him. Refer him to third-party resources, such as books, videos, audiotapes, or Web sites that will answer his questions or remove his doubts regarding the network marketing industry. These resources may be oriented toward your particular company or may be generic, about the MLM industry in general.

Directing him toward such resources gives you a hook for your later follow-up. You can always call your prospect back and ask whether he has taken a look yet at the materials you gave him or referred him to. Stay in touch with your client, no matter what. Six months down the line, he may change his mind. Or if he doesn't, he may eventually lead you to someone with an interest.

HORSES AND WATER

The same principle of relationship-building applies within your downline. Back in chapter 12, we learned how Cindy nearly destroyed a relationship with one of her top leaders by pushing her to do more than she was willing to do. Cindy would not make that mistake today. "I've learned that you can lead a horse to water, but you can't make him drink," she says. "I've learned to have tremendous patience with people. If people want my guidance and ask for it, I'll give it to them. But if they don't take action, I just love them for who they are and continue to work with those who do take action."

Cindy is always hunting for those people, within her downline, who share her passion for action. She goes to her leaders and tells them, "Lead me to the best person you know in your downline." And she works downline as far as she needs to, in order to find those people. "I'm working with people so far down that I don't even get paid on them," she says. "But I love doing it. I know it's helping my organization in the long-run to help them build depth. I want to set fires underneath people."

NO BOSSES

In *The Art of the Leader*, William A. Cohen relates that when Baron Von Steuben arrived to help train George Washington's troops, he was startled by the attitude of America's citizen soldiers. "Back home, I need only say 'Do this,' and the soldier does it," he wrote in a letter. "Here in America, I must also give a good reason for my order. Only then does the soldier do what I say."

Network marketers have a similar attitude. Like the men of the Continental Army, they will stand and fight if the spirit moves them. But if their mood changes, they are just as likely to pack their gear and head home.

"In networking, the investment is not large," says Jerry Campisi. "And people work from the privacy of their homes. There's little overhead and no boss. That's the best part of the business and the worst part of the business. It's the worst part because most people don't have the discipline to work their own hours. So it's part of your job as a leader to create that discipline for them."

THE POWER TO IGNORE

Cindy Samuelson creates discipline through a process of elimination. She bypasses those people who fail to demonstrate drive and commitment. This allows Cindy to focus her energy where it will do the most good. It also sends an unspoken message to the rest of her downline that if they want Cindy's personal attention, they need to get serious about their business.

The power to grant or withhold attention is probably the best leverage you have for getting your "citizen entrepreneurs" to do what you want. Never underestimate its force. But it is also one of the most benign motivators you can use. Bypassing a person might offend, hurt, or even scare him, but it will not humiliate him, as yelling and browbeating would.

THE POWER OF COMPETITION

A more proactive strategy for stirring up sluggish downlines is to harness people's natural competitiveness. Campisi does this through contests. He usually holds them around 10 A.M. on a Saturday. Jerry gathers his group and tells everyone to pair off. He then challenges each pair to go out and try to get leads, through social interaction. The object is to meet people and exchange business cards. The person who has the most cards at the end of the day wins.

Prizes can range from a free dinner to a laptop computer, depending on the size of the group. Jerry says that the increase in sales generated by the contest more than compensates for the value of the prize. "I've seen group volumes jump $5,000 to $10,000 in one day," says Jerry. "You're forcing production. You're getting people to work on a Saturday, when they would otherwise be sitting around at home."

CAPPS REPORT

Another device Jerry uses to "force production" from his group is the CAPPS report. This is a standardized sheet that he asks distributors to fill out voluntarily and send to their upline every Monday. It asks the following questions:

C—How many *contacts* did you make this week?

A—How many *appointments* did you make from those contacts?

P—How many *presentations* did you do from those appointments?

P—How many *products* or services did you sell?

S—How many *sign-ups* did you get?

The CAPPS report serves two functions. First, it helps upline leaders diagnose where their distributors might be having trouble. Are they failing to make contacts? Perhaps they need coaching on prospecting techniques. Are they failing to make appointments from their contacts? Maybe they need to work on their follow-up. Or perhaps they're not selling enough product. Maybe they need to do some product roundtables or home product clinics.

"I know from looking at the report where the person needs work," says Jerry. "Maybe I'll see that he did one presentation but only did two appointments. I'll say, 'Your closing ratio is unbelievable. But you need to get more contacts.' Or 'You're getting plenty of contacts, but only 20 percent of your people are showing up for the appointment.'"

> As a leader, you will always have more drive and ambition than most people in your downline.

An equally important purpose of the CAPPS report, however, is to apply psychological pressure on people to produce. The report is voluntary. No one is obliged to fill it out. But no one wants to turn in a blank sheet every week. Generally, people who are not serious about the business simply don't turn in their reports at all. That immediately alerts the upline not to waste any more time on that person. You don't have to beg, cajole, or pester the person on the phone. You simply note that he doesn't send his reports, and you write him off.

"These are not employees," says Jerry. "You can't force them to do things. But having them fill out a CAPPS report encourages people to have the discipline that's necessary to be successful in this business."

IN THE SPIRIT OF *MUSHIN*

As a leader, you will always have more drive and ambition than most people in your downline. This can lead to tremendous frustration. It can put you in a permanent state of war with your distributors. The unwinnable struggle to force people to produce against their will can drain your energy and embitter your soul. It can turn you into a tyrant.

But if you approach the problem in the spirit of *mushin,* you can get what you want without anger or discord. You can sidestep every roadblock with the grace and fluidity of a judo master.

CHAPTER 18

Strategy Number 4— Be Flexible

Larry Smith got an important lesson when he arrived in Vietnam. No sooner had he stepped off the plane, than he saw body bags being loaded up for the trip home. "I realized that I wasn't sitting at home watching this on TV anymore," he recalls. "This was for real."

Larry got more than his fill of reality as an airborne ranger. After two months in Vietnam, he found it hard to believe that he would ever make it home.

"I had three hundred days left," he says. "It seemed like I'd never get there. It was too far away." The only way to cope with the pressures of combat, Larry realized, was to take it one day at a time. "Every day, I thought about what I was going to do that day to make sure that I stay alive until tomorrow."

FOCUS

Larry was a radio operator. When his unit was on patrol, the enemy could attack at any moment. Larry had to be ready to call in an airstrike or artillery strike. That meant he had to keep track of where his unit was, at all times, according to the grid coordinates on a special laminated map.

It was a huge responsibility. It left no time for ruminating about the future or counting the days until his tour was up. "They say that inch by inch is a cinch, yard by yard is hard," says Larry. "I learned that I could get there by taking baby steps, where you just put one foot in front of the other. I couldn't get too hung up with what was down the road, because it got me out of focus to what I needed to be doing today."

MUSHIN

Larry had discovered his own personal path to *mushin*—that detached state of mind sought by samurai warriors. "Whatever state of mind you are in, ignore it," said the sixteenth-century Japanese sword master Miyamoto Musashi, whom we met in chapter 10. "Think only of cutting."

Larry's predominant emotion in Vietnam was fear. "In the beginning, I was scared to death, and in the end I was scared to death," he recalls. But Larry learned to distance himself from his fear. "There comes an acceptance level, during your tour," says Larry. "I don't want to call it a comfort level, but it's an acceptance level, where you're not looking over your shoulder every two seconds. You're aware of danger, but you're not distracted by it." By the time his tour was up, Larry had mastered his fear. When a friend of his was killed in action, Larry signed on for a second tour, burning with desire to get revenge. Fear was still with him, but it played no role in Larry's decision.

INNER STRENGTH

When he finally returned home after two years in Vietnam, the eighteen-year-old kid who had enlisted was now a twenty-year-old man with a maturity beyond his years. Larry and some of his buddies from his ranger unit made up business cards that said: "We have done so much with so little for so long, we can do anything with nothing forever."

"There's a feeling that if you can get through that, you can get through anything," says Larry. "Everything else becomes a piece of cake." Larry has carried that inner strength with him through a successful business career, first as a corporate executive, then later as a network marketer.

FLEXIBILITY

"The biggest lesson I learned in Vietnam," says Larry, "is an appreciation of life itself. I learned that life can be taken away so quickly, for no specific reason." As a result, Larry shies away from setting rigid goals. "I'm not into short-term or long-term goals," he says. "I'm into today's goals. The last thing I do before I say my prayers at night is sit down and prioritize my next day and say, 'Okay, what are the things that I will do tomorrow that will make the biggest difference in my business?'"

> "**I**'m not into short-term or long-term goals, I'm into today's goals."

Larry moves forward through baby steps, one day at a time, just as he did in the jungles of Vietnam. That approach gives him the flexibility to switch course unexpectedly and react to new developments. "I've seen people get so hung up on their goals that they become oblivious to new opportunities," says Larry. "I always want to have the freedom to take advantage of the best opportunities on a day-in, day-out basis."

A LONG-TERM GOAL

For twenty-seven years, Larry pursued the goal of becoming a company president in corporate America. He marveled at the size of his paycheck for his first entry-level job, and at the fact that he'd been given a company car and expense account. "I thought, 'Man this is such a great deal,'" Larry remembers. "'They're giving me all this and I don't know anything about this company.'"

But Larry soon realized that the company did not give something for nothing. As the years went by, the financial balance shifted slowly in the company's favor. Larry's knowledge and effectiveness increased by hundreds of percentage points each year. Yet his raises never exceeded 5 or 10 percent. "In the long run, they were recouping their investment on my initial expense," says Larry. "Now I was being paid *less* than I was really worth."

AN EMPTY TRIUMPH

Larry tried everything to break out of the rut of linear income. He worked for a number of firms, in sales management positions. He even tried investing in a startup company, losing a fortune in the process. In the end, Larry did manage to achieve his goal of becoming a corporate president. He was put in charge of the U.S. division of an Australian firm. But the company shut down its operations globally after only a year, despite the fact that Larry's division was profitable. He found himself out of a job.

Larry realized that he had stuck too rigidly to his goal of climbing the corporate ladder. Having attained it, he found that goal to be empty. At age forty-five, Larry was facing a dismal future. He quickly incurred over $31,000 in credit card debt. In some ways, he felt that he was back in the jungles of Vietnam, living day to day and moment to moment. The stress was terrible. Yet, the pressure of his situation also served to restore Larry's psychological edge. He remembered once more what it meant to function in a state of *mushin,* where life itself depended upon one's ability to step back, analyze and think clearly, even amid the fury of combat.

PRODUCT DRIVEN

Larry had dabbled with MLM opportunities in years past. He had found it hard going. Many of the products seemed overpriced, and hard to sell. The compensation plans, in some cases, required Larry to make large monthly inventory purchases, just to qualify for decent commissions. Larry believed in the industry, but found the specific opportunities he had tried difficult to work.

Pre-Paid Legal seemed different. It was more of a product-driven company, in Larry's estimation. "They had a product that everybody could afford, that everybody needed, and that basically [at that time] had no competition," Larry observes. Pre-Paid's basic legal insurance package went for only $25 per month in Larry's state. Yet it offered a unique and powerful benefit. Shortly after signing on with Pre-Paid Legal, Larry had a run-in with a jeweler. The man had ruined a ring while trying to repair the band, but now refused to pay for it. Under ordinary circumstances, Larry would have had to walk away. The cost of hiring an attorney would have been greater than the value of the ring. But, with his Pre-Paid Legal coverage, Larry called up a member firm and explained the situation. The lawyer called the jeweler. "The same afternoon that jeweler told me he couldn't help me, he gave me a check for $2,152.32 to pay for the ring, and I never paid more than my $25 monthly premium," says Larry.

PRODUCT OF THE PRODUCT

"I thought 'How many times have I been treated that same way, and couldn't do anything about it?'" Larry recalls. "From that point, I never had any question whether this opportunity would work. It was my conviction that if people just understood what this product did for them, they would want it."

Larry had undergone the mental shift known to network marketers as "becoming a product of the product." He had become a true believer. In the corporate world, Larry had had a hard time finding a product that aroused his passions. One of his best-paying jobs had been director of sales for a liquor company. He had worked that job for six years, but Larry had never felt quite right about pushing people to drink more booze. As a network marketer, he had tried selling skin creams, diet products and long-distance phone service. But only now did Larry's business fill him with the conviction that he could change people's lives for the better.

SAME EFFORT, MORE PAY

Fired with enthusiasm, Larry went to work building his Pre-Paid Legal business. He made $4,000 in his third month—enough to go full time. Larry's first-year earnings were $65,000. He now earns nearly a quarter of a million dollars per year, of which almost $200,000 is passive, residual income. "That's what I make without getting of bed," he says. "That's pretty powerful, after four years of work."

Larry put in fifteen-hour days while building his Pre-Paid Legal business. Yet, in hindsight, he does not believe that he worked harder in network marketing than in the corporate world. "I worked it like I would any other career," he says. "I just performed the same daily discipline of showing up every day, learning the business, building my professional skills. But instead of an annual raise of 5 or 8 percent, I was making many times that."

LOOSE GOAL, TIGHT FOCUS

In chapter 13, we discussed the need to remain flexible in the pursuit of one's vision. As Ed Simon, president of Herman Miller, put it: "When you are immersed in a vision, you know what needs to be done. But you

> The key was remaining flexible, and not allowing his goals to become so rigid or specific that they would keep him from making a mid-course correction, when necessary.

often don't know how to do it. You run an experiment because you think it's going to get you there. It doesn't work. New input. New data. You change direction and run another experiment. Everything is an experiment, but there is no ambiguity at all. It is perfectly clear why you are doing it."

Through trial and error, Larry had hit upon a winning combination. The key was remaining flexible, and not allowing his goals to become so rigid or specific that they would keep him from making a mid-course correction, when necessary. Today, Larry keeps his goals loose and his mind open. As he learned to do in Vietnam, he focuses relentlessly on making each day count. But he is ready, at any moment, to react to new data and new developments and to shift gears when necessary.

STUCK IN A RUT

Leah Singleton turned her business around by striking the perfect balance between discipline and flexibility. As a distributor for Herbalife, she became successful by following the mail-order system promoted by her upline. But after a while, Leah realized that the system was too rigid. "Our response was getting lower," says Leah. "Everything I was reading about mail order said that you had to re-do your mail piece every twelve to twenty-four months. But ours hadn't been updated in two years." Therefore, she decided to develop her own system for her organization.

THE PICKLE CONCEPT

Leah was faced with a dilemma. On the one hand, she could understand her upline's reluctance to change. Her mail-order system had been extremely successful, while it lasted. The natural temptation was to leave it exactly as it was, on the principle of, "If it ain't broke, don't fix it."

In addition, Leah's experience had shown her the value of teamwork. A rare synergy had been achieved by the team, during the months when everyone was following the same game plan. They had followed what Leah calls the "Pickle Concept." In a McDonald's restaurant, Leah explains, "they always put three pickles on the hamburger. Everything is exactly the same. You get a team doing the same thing, and it's going to make everything work smoother, faster and no one's going to be second-guessing what they should be doing, because everybody's doing the same thing." It was precisely when everyone on the team started getting tired of the system and going their own way that the synergy collapsed. "Before, we were using all the same scripts, the same voice mails, the same training tools," says Leah. "And then somehow it faded. The team just broke up. And that's when my check started slowing down more and more, because I had all these leaders who were doing something different."

The Perfect Balance

Leah realized that an effective team would have to provide the perfect balance between freedom and discipline. It would have to retain the "pickle concept," while at the same time giving members the freedom to innovate.

The chance to prove her concept came with the Internet. At a training session, Leah heard John and Susan Peterson, the top distributors in Herbalife, explaining that 90 percent of their business was now coming from Internet promotion. Subsequently, at a convention in Kona, Hawaii, Leah heard the late Mark Hughes—founder of Herbalife—tell the sales force, "The Internet is the next explosion of direct marketing. You guys have got to pay attention."

"This was a guy who got up onstage and did hulas and just had a ball," Leah remembers. "So when he got so quiet and serious, all of a sudden, I had to pay attention."

The E-Team

Leah decided to assemble a leadership team specifically dedicated to building the Herbalife business through the Internet. She called it the E-Team. Members would promote their business online, through Web sites, and encourage their downlines to do likewise.[1] They would also use interactive tools, such as e-mail alerts, CD-ROM cards and online conferencing for leadership training, prospecting and managing their downlines.

Leah made membership on the E-Team voluntary. She gave her leaders a choice whether or not to join. Two of her leaders actually declined, preferring to stick with the mail-order system they already knew. But most were excited about the new opportunity.

FREEDOM AND DISCIPLINE

The key to the E-Team's success was that it allowed members to innovate, without losing the discipline of the "pickle concept." Members were encouraged to experiment with new technologies, sales scripts, and prospecting techniques. But if they found something that worked, they were expected to bring it back to the team, where it would be discussed via teleconference.

> **M**embers were encouraged to experiment with new technologies, sales scripts, and prospecting techniques.

"A lot of times in network marketing, people go off and find their own things and keep it within their organization," says Leah. "But on the E-Team, we encourage people to share all the tools they're using with everyone else." When a technique is clearly shown to improve results, the E-Team adopts it as a group. "So we all end up promoting the same thing," says

---

1. At this writing, Herbalife allows distributors to put up their own Web sites. Many companies, however, require distributors to use only company-supplied or company-designed Web sites. This writer has no way of knowing whether Herbalife may adopt such a policy in future.

Leah. "People in our downlines are hearing the same message from me and from my team leaders. They're hearing that this new method is great, and it's creating excitement, because the whole team is working together. It's the difference between two goats going at it head to head, saying 'I like my script better,' 'No, I like my script better,' and a herd of buffalo running through the prairie, full speed, all running together."

THE POWER OF ALIGNMENT

Leah is talking about the power of alignment, that special synergy that occurs when members of a team adopt a unified vision. The success of the E-Team concept showed up quickly in the numbers. "When you look at my organization, it's the E-Team that's growing, not the people who are doing their own thing," says Leah. "The difference is like night and day, black and white."

Leah points to one E-Team member whose check went up more than 150 percent in two months. "It's been such a short time, and it's already starting to magnify in my group," says Leah. "People are starting to see their checks move like they haven't moved in three years." The key is voluntarism. Leah's E-Team maintains a disciplined, "Three-Pickle" approach not because they are pressured into it, but because they see it working. And anyone who wishes to experiment is still free to do so.

"When you're building a large, multilevel organization," says Leah, "your leaders get to a certain level and they start to have their own ideas that they want to try out. We give people a way of doing that, of going out and testing things, and maybe even failing at them, while still being able to stay on the team."

ADAPTABILITY

For Stan and Donna Colson, calmness under fire and flexibility proved as crucial to their business survival as they had to Larry Smith's literal survival in Vietnam. The Colsons thought they had it made, as distributors for FreeLife, an MLM company with an exclusive license to market the products of vitamin guru Earl Mindell. A mechanical engineer by profession, and a computer nerd by avocation, Stan had pioneered Internet promotion at a time when most MLMers were still figuring out how to use e-mail.

I told the Colsons' story in my 1996 book *The Wave 3 Way to Building Your Downline*. At that time, they were getting a 25 percent sign-up rate from e-mail inquiries through their Web site, and reported that they were making about $4,000 per month. "We eventually had a huge site with about 700 pages," says Donna, "and we were doing virtually all of our business online."

THE SHOCK

Then one day it came to an end. Top management at FreeLife had been watching as other MLM companies were hit with legal and regulatory actions, due to improper product and earnings claims made by individual distributors on their Web sites. So FreeLife decided to play it safe. One day, the company announced that distributors would no longer be allowed to use the FreeLife name or that of Earl Mindell in their Web site promotions. If they advertised on the Web at all, they would have to do so generically.

"It was very disturbing," Donna recalls. "Prospecting on the Web was the only way we knew to do the business. We'd put a lot of blood, sweat and tears into building our online business. It was a real setback." But the Colsons rolled with the punches. "We stood behind the company all the way. We just realized that we would have to learn to build the business the traditional way."

BLESSING IN DISGUISE

For two years, Stan and Donna applied themselves to the demanding tasks of traditional networking: working the warm market; doing three-way calls; holding meetings, and so forth. "It turned out to be a blessing in disguise," says Donna. "The problem with our Web business was that it was hard for people to duplicate." Although the Colsons had done their best to help their people build Web sites, few had the resources or technical expertise to emulate what the Colsons had done.

Now that they were down in the trenches, working their business the old-fashioned way, the Colsons got a feel for the special challenges of meeting and working with people in the flesh. "MLM isn't an easy business to do," says Donna. "We found that out the hard way. You have to run ads and do word of mouth to get people's attention; send them packages; send them another package if they want more information; do follow-up calls, then go back and repeat the process all over again. Traditional MLM is a very hard business. It takes really strong people who can stick with it, with strong personalities and stamina, who won't give up and who will stick with it through the long haul."

BABY STEPS

As Larry Smith had done in Vietnam, the Colsons closed their minds to the awesomeness of the task before them. Trying to imagine all the years of drudgery that lay ahead would have been too discouraging. Instead, they focused on day-to-day tasks. They took baby steps, one at a time. "Financially, we were just treading water," says Donna. "Our business stopped growing for two years."

But they kept alert to opportunity. Whenever they got the chance, the Colsons urged upper management at Free-Life not to forget about the Internet. "We talked about the future of the Internet, how e-commerce was growing by leaps and bounds, and how we needed to take advantage of that," says Donna. But, at the end of the day, the decision was out of their hands. All the Colsons could do was focus on their immediate tasks and wait.

DUPLICABILITY

Their patience paid off in the end. In early 2000, FreeLife rolled out a new Internet program that allowed distributors to prospect on the Web. To manage the legal risks, FreeLife controlled content on its distributors' sites. But each distributor was entitled to a free, fully interactive e-commerce site customized for his or her business. "People can sign up on-line and order products online," Donna explains. "If people sign up through your site, they are automatically put in your downline."

Not only were the Colsons back in business as Web-based distributors, but now they had a system that was truly duplicable. "I can just hand a card to someone and say, 'Hey, go check out this Web site,'" says Donna. "People see how easy it is to just order something and add it to their shopping cart, like on Amazon.com."

Stan has put his expertise to work making the system even more user-friendly for his downline. He has created a "front page" that acts as a guided tour or mentor, helping visitors navigate more easily through the complexities of the FreeLife site and showing them how to order products and sign up as distributors. "Now that I'm in the mode of doing business the traditional MLM way, face to face, it's easier for me to teach people this new way of doing business," says Donna. "For the first time, people can really just sit in front of a computer and do this business. I never believed that was possible before, for most people."

Like Larry Smith when he returned from Vietnam, the Colsons feel that they have done so much with so little for so long, that they can now do almost anything with nothing. New challenges face them everyday. But they have learned to face each one in the serene but flexible spirit of *mushin*.

CHAPTER 19

Strategy Number 5— Partner Up

O ne thing that's interesting about being a leader," says Ken Porter, a leading distributor for Usana, "is that as you grow bigger, everyone's problems start becoming your problems. When you're just starting out, the only person you have to take care of is yourself. But once you get big, everyone leans on you. If they have a problem, they bring it to you. That's one of the most difficult things about this business."

To some extent, dealing with people's problems is part of your responsibility as a leader. But many of the calls you'll get from your downline won't be about real problems. They will be from people who need emotional encouragement to keep them going through the day. One of your key challenges as a leader is to find a way to meet these emotional needs without allowing them to drain your time and energy. Encouraging your downline to partner up is one of the most effective.

COUPLE POWER

Feminist Gloria Steinem once said "A woman needs a man like a fish needs a bicycle." In real life, however, men and women need each other very badly. Married couples not only live longer, but also succeed more readily in business. Savvy networkers have long taken advantage of this principle by targeting married couples for recruitment. When couples work the business together, they look to each other for much of the daily support and encouragement that they would otherwise seek from their upline.

Of course, some people are not married. And others have spouses whose minds are so closed to the business, that there is no hope of recruiting them. Nutrition for Life distributors David and Shannon Biegel have developed a technique for dealing with such situations. Those in their downline who do not have a supportive spouse, for whatever reason, are encouraged to choose a "running mate" with whom they can team up to work the business.

> Married couples not only live longer, but also succeed more readily in business.

A WINNING TEAM

David and Shannon met through the Nutrition for Life business. David was a successful eye doctor in Montana who had gone on to become an even more successful network marketer. David would travel from city to city in Montana, doing presentations at business meetings. A friend of Shannon's invited her to see David speak at one of those meetings and, as Shannon puts it, "It was love at first sight."

A successful travel agent, Shannon was nonetheless looking for better opportunities, and she joined Nutrition for Life shortly after. She and David were married within a year. They made a powerful team. David focused mainly on motivating and inspiring people, through his presentations at business meetings. Shannon spent most of her time down in the trenches, doing the day-to-day prospecting and downline management, by phone and e-mail. "Together we became one of the first five-star Platinums in the company, which at that time was the highest level of achievement," says Shannon. "My husband was able to retire from being an eye doctor, and I retired from my travel business."

UNSUPPORTIVE SPOUSES

Despite their success, David and Shannon never outgrew their need for constant emotional support. "If I'm on the phone and I get four or five no's in a row, that can get me down," she says. "I need to hear David tell me once more that it's a numbers game and I just need to hang in there. Even though I already know it, it helps me to hear it from him."

But the Biegels found that others in their downline did not enjoy the same kind of mutual support. "People would come up and tell us, 'I feel so alone. I don't feel part of the group,'" says Shannon. These people were often married, but had spouses who disapproved of the business, or perhaps were simply apathetic toward it. Rather than resigning themselves to losing such people, the Biegels began instituting a buddy system to keep them on track.

RUNNING MATES

In one case, David and Shannon noticed one woman in their downline who seemed to be losing her enthusiasm for the business. She was coming to meetings less and less often. It turned out that she was feeling dejected and left out. Her husband was not opposed to her MLM business, but he had no interest in it. So the woman had nowhere to go when she needed encouragement.

David and Shannon encouraged her to team up with a running mate. She found another married woman crossline from her, whose husband was also unsupportive. The two women began driving to meetings together, doing two-on-ones with prospects, and traveling together to out-of-town meetings. Before long, both had risen to substantial leadership positions in the group.

"It's beneficial to work as a couple," says Shannon. "I believe everybody needs a running mate, somebody there to encourage them, counsel them and communicate with them."

The Five Core Strategies of MLM Leadership: Summary

STRATEGY NUMBER 1—BUILD A TEAM

At the outset of the Civil War, Abraham Lincoln formulated a plan to strike the Southern armies aggressively and repeatedly until they were annihilated. Yet none of his generals shared this vision. Their strategies were timid and defensive. Lincoln went through many different commanders before finally settling on Ulysses S. Grant. But once Grant was in charge, things moved quickly. Because he was a fighter, Grant attracted other fighters to his team, such as William Tecumseh Sherman. Only a year after Grant was given command of the Union Army, the war was over. It might have ended a lot sooner, had Grant been appointed at the very beginning of the conflict. The moral of the story—as David Phillips avers in *Lincoln on Leadership*—is that, in building a team, you must keep searching until you find your Grant. Once your

"Grant" is in place, he will attract others of like mettle. And your downline will begin to grow quickly.

STRATEGY NUMBER 2—TRAIN YOUR PEOPLE

At some point in any network marketing business, you will wake up one morning and say to yourself, "Who am I going to talk to today?" You have run out of prospects. Many networkers quit the business at this point, not because they are lazy or fainthearted, but simply because they do not know what to do next. Your job as a leader is to intervene at this point and provide prospecting alternatives.

STRATEGY NUMBER 3—LEAD BY PERSUASION

As a leader, you will always have more drive and ambition than most people in your downline. Often you will be tempted to pressure and browbeat your people, even to lose your temper with them. But such methods will never get the results you want. Persuasion is more effective than force. A leader must learn to temper his emotions. He must attain *mushin*—a detached state of mind known to the ancient samurai, in which you study your opponent and redirect his aggression in the midst of combat. With calmness and deliberation, you can apply the principles of persuasive leadership to gain the cooperation of even the most stubborn and intractable of your distributors.

STRATEGY NUMBER 4—BE FLEXIBLE

Keep your goals loose, and don't be afraid to change them when the situation warrants it.

STRATEGY NUMBER 5—PARTNER UP

As your organization grows, people in your downline will lean on you more and more. Everyone's problems will become your problems. Many of the calls you get from your downline will not be about real problems however. They will be from people who need emotional encouragement to get through the day. One way to lessen these emotional demands is to recruit couples and encourage them to work as a team, so they will support each other. Unmarried people, or people with unsupportive spouses can be encouraged to partner up with "running mates."

Conclusion:
The Test of Leadership

Not long ago, Pre-Paid Legal distributor Art Jonak returned from a nineteen-day cruise in the Caribbean. As he stepped into his office, Art braced himself for the barrage. Generally, when he returned from a long trip, he could expect to find forty to fifty panicky messages from his downline clogging up his voice mail.

Most of them would be "What-should-I-do?" questions. Someone might say, "Art, we just had a meeting here in California and Tom didn't do the meeting, Cindy did, and well, Cindy didn't do such a good job with the product presentation and that's why a lot of prospects didn't sign up. What should I do?" or "Art, we submitted an application to the home office and it didn't go through. They say it got lost. What should I do?"

For the life of him, Art could not understand why intelligent people could not figure out how to handle many of these problems themselves. But he also knew that holding people's hands was part of what it meant to be a leader. So when he entered his office that day, Art resigned himself to being inundated by the usual battery of "What-should-I-do?" questions.

THE BUFFER

Yet miraculously, it didn't happen. Art found only six messages waiting for him. And the messages were mostly positive. They were from people saying things like, "Listen, Art, we've got a great prospect here who's serious about joining the business, and I've gotten him to a point where he really needs to talk to you directly." Art sank down in his chair and breathed a huge sigh of relief. It had finally happened. His Magic Moment had arrived.

There was only one explanation for the small number of messages. Other people must be fielding the questions. Leaders in Art's downline had begun running interference for him. They were solving their own problems and answering the questions that filtered up from their downlines.

Art had been dreaming of this moment for over a year. That's how long it had taken him to recruit and train a core group of leaders, capable of running the business on their own. But now his efforts had paid off. With a deep sense of satisfaction, Art realized that his life would be a lot less frantic from now on. It would also be more profitable. When his next commission check arrived, Art found that his monthly income had risen by nearly $4,000.

THE LEADERSHIP TEST

"A leader is someone who handles problems," says Art. "Let's say Carlos has a problem with an order. He calls his upline and says the home office lost his order. Now that leader can do one of two things. He can call me up and say, 'Art, what should I do?' Or he can call the home office himself and put a trace on the order, and then call Carlos back and calm him down, explain to him that the home office is run by human beings, and reassure him that his order will be found and processed.

"That's the leadership test. The test is, will you handle the problem yourself, or will you let it filter upline to the next guy? That's the test that separates the leaders from the crowd. It separates the true leaders from those people who just think they're leaders but don't act like leaders."

DESIRE

Like Generals Dwight Eisenhower and William Tecumseh Sherman, Art firmly believes that leaders are made rather than born. People must be taught how to lead a network marketing organization. But before that teaching process can begin, they must demonstrate that they have the desire. Art has found that he can tell right away which of his recruits are worth training for leadership and which are not.

"I give people a quick leadership test," he says. "I give them a book about network marketing. Any book. And I say, I want you to read this book, and we'll talk about it Monday. Then I call up next week and ask, 'Did you read the book?' Some people will say, 'Well, no, the football game was on.' That person is not ready for leadership. But then someone else won't even wait for my call. He'll call me on Sunday, and say, 'That book was awesome. Let's get together soon.'"

Such people will not be daunted, later on in the training process, if you phone them at the last minute and say, "Listen, I can't make it to the meeting. You're going to have to run things on your own." On the contrary, they will be eager for the chance to run things themselves.

YOU'VE GOT TO SWING, TO MAKE HOME RUNS

It is no coincidence that the baseball players who set the records for home runs also tend to be the ones who strike out most often. That is because they are not afraid to swing the bat with all their might. Taking a swing is risky. It can go either way. But it is also the essence of leadership. You must be willing to risk defeat if you hope to gain victory.

In the final analysis, there is no formula for becoming a leader, no system or strategy that will guarantee the result.

There is only that split-second moment of decision as the ball comes whizzing in over the plate. Will you take a chance and swing? Or will you play it safe? On that decision hangs the difference between the leaders and the followers.

INDEX

Wells, Gary
  mission of, 55–56
  Missouri mule principle of, 55
  negative spouse of, 54–55
  retirement of, 53
  as role model, 48–49
Wells, Rebecca, 54, 56
"What-should-I-do?" questions,
  193, 194
White Castle, 108
Work, treating as a game, 64, 67,
  97

X
Xenophon, 80–81, 82

Y
Yearbooks as memory joggers, 121

Z
Ziglar, Zig, 5